Dream

on

Purpose !

signature

Advance Praise for **Profit with Purpose**

To see full quotes go to www.paramountbooks.com

[A] multicultural marketing manifesto. Teneshia's insight into servant-style leadership as the essential underpinning to the success of accomplished marketers is refreshing.
> —**Adrianne C. Smith,** CEO/Managing Partner, AdHere Network; formerly, Executive Director Center for Excellence in Advertising, Howard University

Ms. Warner has successfully sewn together a collection of anecdotes and case studies that reflect branding with purpose, a hallmark of the new economy and a guiding principle for the creativity and ideas that drive it.
> —**Richie Cruz,** Lifestyle Marketing Specialist, Pepsi-Cola North America Beverages

Profit with Purpose vividly highlights how a brand can emotionally connect to the fast-growing multicultural segment. . . . provides invaluable contemporary knowledge to foster relationships with this key demographic.
> —**Karmetria Burton,** Vice President, Supplier Diversity, Delta Airlines

This book helped me understand the purpose of my brand in consumers' lives, and how a meaningful purpose can drive business growth . . .
> —**Tommy Hillman,** General Mills, Brand Manager, Box Tops For Education, Multicultural Marketing

The chapter on selecting the right community partners for your brand is "spot on." A must read!
> —**Iasha Rivers,** Director of External Affairs and Corporate Communications, Macy's Inc.

. . . multicultural marketing campaigns "don't mean a thing if they ain't got that swing." And that swing, in this case, is purpose. Mrs. Warner connects the dots between profits and purpose. I give it six doo-wops.
> —**Alonzo Byrd,** Assistant Vice President, Public Affairs, Enterprise Holdings

Teneshia . . . has chosen to passionately advocate for a new kind of personal wealth-that is to encourage executives to work with "purpose."
> —**Andrea Hoffman,** Founder & CEO, Diversity Affluence

This book delivers! It inspires us all to create brands and consumer relationships that get it right.
> —**Cheryl Walker-Robertson,** Executive Vice President, Odyssey Media

As an entrepreneur this book spoke to me in a very real way. I look to partner with companies that "have a soul." . . . a must read for any business looking to authentically connect with their clients.
> —**Brandice Henderson,** CEO & Founder, Harlem's Fashion Row

Profit with Purpose speaks to a core value to profit *with, not from,* the communities and clients you serve. Kudos!
> —**Tiffany R. Warren,** Senior VP, Chief Diversity Officer, Omnicom Group; President, ADCOLOR

. . . a thoughtful blend of case studies, data, interesting anecdotes, and distilled takeaways that make it an engaging and valuable read.
> —**Heide Gardner,** Chief Diversity & Inclusion Officer, Interpublic Group

. . .this book hits the core of purpose right where we all need it. It informs, educates, and excites . . .
> —**Sandra Sims-Williams,** SVP, People Insights & Inclusion, Publicis Groupe – VivaKi

I've learned from Teneshia that when passion and purpose meet, amazing things can happen for not only brands, but for people. Congratulations!
> —**Laura Hall,** Managing Director, Global Consumer & Brand Marketing Practice, Burson-Marsteller

. . . an absolute "must read" for all serious marketers. Open the book to any page and there is applicable wisdom—varied and inspiring.
> —**Mike Hemingway,** Founder and CEO, Brand Hunger

. . . provides the insights, step-by-step tools and engaging case studies demonstrating how to connect with this audience in a purposeful way.
>—**Sandra Krut,** CSW, Brand Director, BANFI Vinters – Rosa Regale

Teneshia has analyzed and provided clear direction for building a brand—campaigns and programming that serve a multicultural audience.
>—**Gracia Walker,** AVP Global Communications, Kiehl's Since 1851

If you buy only one book this year to help you go to the next level this is the one. This approach to business and civic life represents a blueprint for sustained success and our nation's best hope for revitalization.
>—**Michael Jones-Bey,** Director, Supplier Diversity, Consolidated Edison

[A] must read for business leaders who are seeking to connect and win with all consumers, especially multicultural consumers.
>—**Najoh Tita-Reid,** Global Strategy Realization & Capability Leader, Merck Consumer Care; founding Brand Marketer, P&G's My Black is Beautiful

[O]ffers a refreshing take on the positive cultural impact the entertainment industry can have in our community.
>—**Marve Frazier,** Chief Creative Officer and CEO, Moguldom Media Group, Bossip.com

. . . designed to help leaders understand that by consistently "enriching" the lives of others—current and potential customers—you virtually guarantee that it is not only possible to do well by doing good, but that behaving in this manner is vital to any organization.
>—**Darryl Cobbin,** Managing Partner, Diamond Diaspora Media

This groundbreaking book highlights the positive contributions the Hip Hop industry makes to support the community that supports them. It demonstrates how brands can harness the influence of Hip Hop artists to enable them to add true value to their target audience. . . . essentially a "manual" on how to connect with the multicultural audience.
>—**L. Londell McMillan,** Esq., CEO & Chairman, NorthStar Group

As inspiring as Teneshia's personal story of struggle and perseverance is, she also understands how to turn those experiences (and the knowledge gained) into profit with purpose. The tips provided realign the skills of seasoned industry veterans and instruct rookies on how to move correctly for a prosperous career path. Life lessons with tough love notes attached.
>—**Datwon Thomas,** Executive Editor, VIBE Media

[A] manual that shows how brands, entertainers and celebrities connect with the community in a way that adds true value and elevates the lives of African Americans. . . . relevant and well overdue.
>—**Mercedes Funderburk**, Director of Talent, BET Networks

. . . inspiration for those who want to strive for their passion, walk in faith, and stick to their purpose, in order to lead to a successful career as well as a balanced, abundant life.
>—**Christina Hardy,** Integrated Marketing, *Essence*

From celebrity endorsements to innovations in social media, Profit with Purpose is a powerful tool that educates, inspires and can ultimately drive measurable results for your brand.
>—**Rachel Strauss-Muñiz,** Marketing & Promotions, *People en Español*

Teneshia's unique approach to cause marketing and ability to align messaging with brand personalities are best in class.
>—**Kimora Lee Simmons,** Designer, Entrepreneur & Philanthropist

. . a much needed analysis and strategic plan for any in the field of marketing and communications, and for those who aspire to enter these fields. . . . written with clarity and humor; universal and sound. This is a must read for communications students everywhere.
>—**Jannette L. Dates,** Dean Emerita, Howard University; Minority Media & Telecom Council Hall of Fame Inductee

Profit with Purpose

A Marketer's Guide to Delivering Purpose-Driven Campaigns to Multicultural Audiences

Teneshia Jackson Warner

Paramount Market Publishing, Inc.

Paramount Market Publishing, Inc.
950 Danby Road, Suite 136
Ithaca, NY 14850
www.paramountbooks.com
Phone: 607-275-8100; 888-787-8100
Fax: 607-275-8101

Publisher: James Madden
Editorial Director: Doris Walsh

Cataloging in Publication Data available
ISBN-10: 0-9851795-0-3 | ISBN-13: 978-0-9851795-0-2

Cover image
  Photographer: JLC Photography
  Makeup Artist: Joanna Simkin
  Fashion Stylist: Marcus Ivory

Contents

Foreword

By Russell Simmons

Chairman, RUSH Communications

I FIRST MET TENESHIA JACKSON several years ago at the Magic Fashion Show in Las Vegas. The meeting was a brief one—Teneshia approached me and explained that she had just left her job at IBM and was looking to pursue something connected to her love of hip-hop music and fashion. Were there, she wondered, any opportunities available in my organization?

I told her that unfortunately there weren't openings at the moment, but that perhaps something might open up in the future and then kept it moving. Most people would have interpreted my response, both verbally and physically, as a "no," but not Teneshia.

I found that out several weeks later at the Global Diversity Summit in Miami. I had just finished addressing the Summit and asked the audience if anyone had additional questions for me. Up rose Teneshia, who in front of a full audience once again offered to serve any of the programs I was working on. And once again, I told her that while I appreciated her attitude and courage, there just weren't any openings.

If the majority of people would have given up after our first conversation, almost everyone would quit after the second. Especially after I said "no" in public. But not Teneshia.

Indeed, when I showed up for work one day in New York City several weeks later, there was Teneshia standing outside of my office, still looking to serve. I explained that nothing had changed on my end, but Teneshia still refused to be discouraged. For the next several days, when I went to work, there was Teneshia. And when I left, Teneshia was still standing there. Still looking to serve.

Finally, after four days of silent but steady persistence on her part, I went over and said, "I can't believe you're still out here. We still don't have any positions open, but if you want to work for free, then come on upstairs and we'll figure something out." So Teneshia jumped on the elevator with me and immediately started serving with enthusiasm. In quick order she worked her way up the ladder in my organization, working on projects such as the "Hip Hop Reader," and the Hip-Hop Summit Action Network *Get Out the Vote* campaign. Despite coming in on the ground floor, Teneshia established herself as one of the true leaders within my organization. Yet she would have never been able to *lead* if she hadn't stood in front of my office for four days in a row looking to *serve* first.

That's why I shared Teneshia's incredibly inspiring story in my book *Do You!* to reflect the maxim that "You Can Never Get Before You Give." Teneshia understood what a lot of people seem to have a difficult time grasping: If you see someone with something *you* like, instead of asking for some of it, help *them* make some more of it. Contribute to their process and help it grow, until eventually you become part of that process yourself. Or to put it even more plainly, "Don't ask for a blessing, be a blessing."

It's so encouraging to see Teneshia use this book to spread the message that there is tremendous value in service. While some mistakenly believe that "serving" somehow connotes belittling or "playing" yourself, I know this book will help people see that service is in fact incredibly empowering. It's not an exaggeration to say that I've based my entire career on the concept that "you must give in order get" and I know that Teneshia has as well.

There isn't a profession or hustle in which service isn't the most valuable trait a person can possess. Even the President of the United States can only be a great leader once he or she proves to be a giving servant first.

So whether you are an aspiring entrepreneur looking for your first break, a professional looking to take your career to the next level or even a CEO trying to figure out how to help your brand provide the world with a lasting and positive service, I encourage you to take Teneshia's message to heart and apply it to all your endeavors.

Because when you can follow Teneshia's example and stay committed to the practice of "giving instead of getting," it won't be long before you become extremely attractive to the world. No matter who you are or what you do.

Foreword

By Renee Wilson

President, MSLGROUP North America

I'VE LONG RESPECTED Teneshia Jackson as a smart and motivated businesswoman. Much of the success of the diversity marketing business partnership between MSLGROUP North America and her firm, EGAMI, is due to the personal persistence and leadership she brings to our work together.

At the 2009 ADCOLOR Awards, Teneshia challenged marketers not only to deliver programs that served multicultural consumers, but to imagine and build campaigns that addressed the true needs of these communities. Our firms' collaboration across a series of programs had raised more than a million dollars in grants, scholarships, and donations to community organizations serving multicultural communities. While she celebrated the business success we achieved together, her satisfaction in also having delivered work with a higher purpose, put extra special sparkle in her eyes. For those of us at MSLGROUP who worked closely with her, Teneshia has become an inspiring woman who understands that marketing success often comes a deep understanding of people combined with a higher purpose.

It has been on this principle that we built our business partnership. Years ago, in some of our first meetings together with Teneshia, my colleagues and I became acquainted with a determination woven through her DNA. Her interpretation of the word "no," for example, means "not now." Through persistence, hard work, and drive, she believes, all things will be possible.

As President of MSLGROUP North America, I lead Publicis Groupe's flagship strategic communication and engagement network in this part of the world. We're approached with a fair share of opportunities for partnerships. Many organizations seek to leverage the expertise of our more than 3500 people in our 100 global offices worldwide that have helped us become one of the top four global PR networks. We have to be skeptical. But, Teneshia got through to us.

With focus and determination, she set out to convince us that EGAMI's multicultural expertise could add great value to our offerings. She spoke to the issue of diversity, one that we fully embraced as a firm, but were seeking unique approaches to underscore our commitment.

We understood Teneshia's point about how multicultural audiences are currently on target to become the new majority in America. And, that as multicultural populations rapidly rise, brands are placing a high priority on engaging these consumers. We engaged in a dialogue about how the multicultural market is quickly increasing its influence on mainstream culture through fashion, music, dance, cuisine and more,

We discussed how the consumers who populate this culture are younger, more acculturated and more tech-savvy. How, with tremendous buying power, multicultural consumers refuse to be ignored. These multicultural consumers can be called the new mainstream, Teneshia suggested. They are using mainstream media, social media and mobile devices more than the general market. Traditional marketing methods are rendered irrelevant in reaching them with the impact that's needed, she pointed out. We agreed.

Teneshia articulated the argument that the growing diversity interests would drive not only the internal workforce, but also product development and consumer marketing communications. After just a few meetings, we were convinced EGAMI's diversity offering would broadly open up a potent channel we could leverage on behalf of our clients. We had, after all, built our MSLGROUP North America diversity approach around client solutions. We understood that these client solutions must come from a deep understanding of the people who comprise the new multicultural face of America. But we also understood to break through, more was required. With her contagious passion, Teneshia was not deterred. She insisted that together we could deliver culturally relevant programs that not only exceeded client objectives, but programs and campaigns that *inspire purpose.* That we fully understood.

So, in 2008, MSLGROUP Americas formed an official strategic alliance for EGAMI to serve as a diversity partner. Since that time, we have worked together with Fortune 100 /500 brands to deliver purpose-inspired campaigns to multicultural audiences. Within a short period of time, our joint work was recognized and received multicultural campaign industry awards from PRWeek, the PRSA Silver Anvil, PRSA NY Big Apple, PRSA Georgia Phoenix Award, Holmes Group Sabre Award, ADCOLOR Awards and more. The success of our work together stems from a critical understanding of multicultural people and a commitment to purpose: People + Purpose. To that end, I am thrilled with our decision to partner and our ability to deliver culturally insightful world-class work that really matters.

As I got to know Teneshia, I came to better understand that her journey to influence and drive innovative campaigns that make a real difference in our world is powered by her own deep sense of personal purpose.

I look forward to MSLGROUP North America continuing to partner with Teneshia. And, it is my hope that this book will serve as inspiration and a resource guide for you to follow Teneshia's lead to deliver your brand *purpose* in all that you do.

Introduction

MARKETING AND MAKING A DIFFERENCE IN THE WORLD—just how compatible are these two objectives? Does the average marketer, already burdened with the need to drive sales and ROI, really care about impacting society? The answer is yes, and it's the driving force behind this book. I believe that the marketing world has just begun to scratch the surface of its power to affect positive change—not just in the lives of consumers but throughout the world. Thus, the goal of this book is not just to instruct, but to inspire. It is also my conviction that it will become an inspiring resource guide for the kind of marketing-change vehicles that give birth to a new discipline in the marketing mix—*Purpose-Inspired Marketing* versus *Inspiration-Driven Marketing,* the art of marketing with a higher purpose. This is not simply "feel good," or nice to do. This is the expectation of today's consumer. Large majorities in the U.S., China, Sweden, and the U.K. say a company can be financially successful by having a higher purpose beyond making money. We have entered a time in which marketers are being asked to push beyond the traditional "four Ps" (product, price, place, and promotion) to a higher one—purpose.

First, I'd like to thank you for choosing this book. Whoever you are—an entrepreneur or small business owner, an organization, a Fortune 500 brand, or just a person with an amazing idea—the ideas here will feed you. The premise of marketing deals with identifying and meeting human and social needs. Marketing is typically seen as the task of creating, promoting, and delivering goods and services to consumers and businesses. Thus, as you aim to provide goods or services to others, you must first be clear on your brand purpose. My goal is to provide you with essential steps and strategies for bringing your brand purpose to life so that you enrich the lives of others in meaningful ways, and profit in the process. Consumers today understand that business needs to make a profit. But they also believe—unilaterally around the world—that business should be doing this in a purposeful way. So no longer are purpose and profit mutually exclusive; they actually go hand in hand. Okay, but just what, you may be wondering, is a purpose-driven marketer?

At its core, the concept is that people, products, and services have a meaning and that meaning is their purpose. And, when that purpose is aligned to meet the needs of others or to serve them, great things can happen. Lives are enriched. Innovation occurs. The world can be improved, and yes, great profits are also possible. This approach to marketing requires us to "get out of the selling business and into the business of helping others be successful." After all, as Roy Spence so eloquently put it in an online article, "People are not going to do business with companies that aren't in the business to make their lives better."[1] This book is all about your brand having a purpose and meaning in the lives of others. And not just that, but a purpose that improves and enhances the lives of others.

Profit With Purpose also sums up my own personal story and search for meaning over the past ten years. Ironically, as I explored my personal meaning and purpose, my journey serendipitously provided me with the opportunity to align and work with brands to serve a purpose in the lives of multicultural audiences. I've had the incredible blessing of learning about urban culture and multicultural audiences across a wide swath of society, of learning from a truly cutting-edge perspective about these audiences and about what is most important to them. The more I learn, the better equipped I am to connect brands to them in meaningful ways. My goal now is to share with you some knowledge and insights gained in the course of this ten-year journey. You will walk away from this book with the following:

- An understanding of purpose-driven marketing
- An overview of multicultural and urban consumers, i.e., what they care about, what matters to them most, and how best to "serve" this market and their community. This is really important since multicultural audiences are the fastest growing U.S. demographic, soon to be the new mainstream. Think about these statistics: The number of racial or ethnic minority persons living the U.S. (according to the 2010 census) was 111,927,986.[2] That represents 36 percent of the total population, or roughly one in every three people, broken down as follows:

	number	percent of the total population
Hispanics or Latinos	50,477,594	16 percent
Blacks or African Americans	37,685,848	12 percent
Asian Americans	14,465,124	5 percent
Other races	3,332,939	1 percent
Two or more races	5,966,481	2 percent

You will learn how your brand can leverage purpose or cause to build advocacy among multicultural and urban consumers. And, you will hear from some of the celebrities who are passionately connecting brands with multicultural audiences.

One truth I have learned is that marketers have a unique power to create change, one idea, product, or campaign at a time. My desire is that marketers will not only be proud of their profession but inspired to use their power constructively, and that this book will serve as an awakening call to that "purpose-driven marketer" within.

As marketers, we deliver products, communication, advertisements, content, and campaigns that engage millions of people daily. According to the *Consumer Reports* website, the average American is bombarded with about 247 commercial messages each day, an estimate that strikes me as being on the low side. Indeed, marketers influence everything from thoughts to desires, from buying decisions to the everyday choices of just about everyone, and the results of our work can be found in every home. That's great power if you ask me!

Take a step back. Look around. You are surrounded by products and services, some of which you consciously chose to purchase, and others that may have been unconsciously selected. Your purchase decisions are thoroughly integrated into your daily life. Some products and or services support you in raising your family; some provide a sense of self-worth and achievement; others help you to experience life's pleasures; and some even support you in making a difference in your community. Think about it: Your life's journey to date reflects an array of product choices that were influenced by a marketer. Therefore, if you're a marketer who thinks that referring to yourself as "one with great powers" is a gross exaggeration, think again! In fact, do more than that: *Awaken.*

Who influences what the world looks like, experiences, and becomes? You do. By the same token, you influence what the world does *not* look like, experience, or become. How amazing is that? Each day, you have the power to go to work and create and influence what is to be made manifest. To some extent the world as we experience it is nothing more than marketer's realized imagination.

As a small business owner, entrepreneur and marketer myself (and CEO of EGAMI Consulting Group), I freely admit that I experience a high in seeing the life cycle of an idea, product, concept, or campaign brought to fruition. I love participating in the process wherein a concept grows from a single idea to a full-blown campaign that engages thousands, if not millions, of people. Take a moment to imagine the possibilities if all marketers were to operate at a level where they were fully aware of their power to do good in the world through their work. Imagine them regarding the gift of marketing as a vessel to impact positive change. Imagine a little more: What if every marketer were intentional about bringing forth products, ideas, experiences, events, information, advertising, communications, and platforms that:

- Shed light on overlooked issues?

- Support consumers in sharing ideas?

- Enhance communities nationwide?

- Build one-on-one relationships with consumers and partnered with them to do good works?

- Address the inequalities in the world?

- Bring humor and laughter to consumers?

- Inspire consumers?

- Support consumers in living their best lives?

- Enrich the lives of their customers?

These can be the results when marketers connect with their inner *purpose-driven* marketer.

When my team and I determined our desire to support brands in creating marketing strategies that would result in a three-tier win-win-win among Brand, Consumer, and Community, it was imperative that each campaign had purpose and in some way contributed to improving the world. Five years later, EGAMI Consulting Group and our strategic agency partner, MSLGROUP, have worked with clients to deliver inspiring brand programs within multicultural communities. While these campaigns have resulted in over a million dollars in scholarships and grants directly affecting those same communities, they also made me realize that, as marketers, we occupy a unique position to impact change in this world of ours.

So, let me ask you, one marketer to another: What mark will you leave? What consumer problem will you solve? How will you impact a consumer's life? Who will you inspire? How many consumers will you empower to make a difference? I believe these are grounding questions that should be considered at the start of each marketing campaign concept. After all, purpose-inspired engagement is the future of marketing. In a recent survey, 87 percent of consumers polled agreed that "business needs to place at least equal weight on society's interests" as it does on its own. And this transcends merely giving out checks to charities. Sixty-two percent agreed that it's "no longer enough for corporations to give money; they must integrate good causes into their everyday business." As well, 63 percent of respondents stated that they "expect brands to donate a portion of their profits to support a good cause."[4] According to the MS&L Global Values Study (conducted in partnership with GfK Roper Public Affairs and Media):

[P]rice and quality are still prime drivers when consumers decide what to buy and from whom. Yet consumers want more, particularly from leading companies. In our increasingly digital world, consumers have more tools to access information about companies and more channels to monitor and hold companies accountable. Ever vigilant, consumers actively watch for signs that companies share their personal values and for warnings that companies fail to practice what they preach. And take heed: Every action, every interaction and every communication is evidence.

Fully 76 percent of Blacks and Hispanics[5] *expect* the leading companies to use social media to connect consumers with others who share similar interests. The opportunity for brands is to create captivating forums through which multicultural consumers can connect and share compelling brand experiences. Or, as Michael Presson, SVP, Digital Strategist for MSLGROUP puts it, "Know your audience—where, what, how they share."

Over the course of this book, as you explore ways your brand can become purpose driven, I'd also challenge you to make this a personal journey. Are you purpose led in your daily life? What's your contribution—is it creativity, great ideas, innovative business strategies, or something else? Connect with how your role enhances and improves the lives of others and, then, connect with your personal purpose. I'd venture to say that behind every purpose-driven brand is a purpose-inspired leader, entrepreneur, marketer, creative, or team. Just as marketers deliver on brand purpose, you have the opportunity to deliver on personal meaning and "life purpose."

If you are creative, connect with the emotion your advertising will evoke within the customer. If your purpose is to inspire, it should be felt in the advertising.

If you are a copywriter, connect with the words and how they empower your consumer. A famous example occurred when Carol H. Williams (founder of the agency of the same name) wrote the famous slogan for Secret deodorant: "Strong enough for a man, but made for a woman." What feeling did she impart to female consumers? It is your purpose as a copywriter to inspire through words.

If you are an entrepreneur launching a new idea, connect with how that idea serves your customer. Is that service your purpose? As we go through this process and examine brand purpose, I encourage you to look at your personal purpose, too, as they are both connected, giving meaning not only to your customer but also to your own life.

Now, let's get ready to go on a journey where it's my hope that you will be enriched as a marketer and that the result of your ideas and great work enrich the lives of the recipients.

Notes

1. www.btobonline.com/article/20110602/STRATEGY02/306029992/bma-annual-purpose-inspired-marketing-crucial-to-winning-business#seenit

2. U.S. Census Bureau 2010, http://factfinder2.census.gove/faces/nav/jsf/pages/index.xthml

3. David Burgos, and Ola Mobolade, *Marketing to the New Majority: Strategies for a Diverse World.* New York: Palgrave Macmillan, 2011.

4. http://www.adweek.com/news/advertising-branding/consumers-expect-better-marketers-103821

5. 2010 MLSGROUP Social Media Survey & Urban Influencer Panel series.

Chapter 1

Dreams with a Purpose

So Remember . . .
You know very well who you are
Don't let 'em hold you down, reach for the stars
　　　　　　　　　　　　　　—Notorious B.I.G., "Juicy"

WHAT DO JAY-Z, OPRAH WINFREY, RICHARD BRANSON, and the late Steve Jobs have in common? They mastered the same thing: the art of dreaming with purpose. The idea of "dreaming" is grounded in a great vision that is inclusive, unconstrained, and expansive. To have purpose is to have meaning, and a reason for existence. To dream with purpose is to combine great vision with meaning and a reason for existence. Thus, it is no surprise that these legendary innovators are the masterminds behind brands that have revolutionized their categories—brands that have provided great meaning and purpose to the world. There's a direct correlation between their life's purpose and their brands—so much so that purpose is truly *interwoven* with their brands. They have each figured out why they exist. More importantly, they have figured out how to align that meaning to the meet the needs of others. They have each defined their purpose and gone on to build powerful brands with *purpose* at their foundation. I imagine that, if they shared their personal purpose statement, it would go something like this:

I am Jay-Z (Shawn Carter) and my brand purpose is to inspire through poetry and expression. I enrich the lives of others through rhymes with high stakes riding on every word and filling every pause with pressure and possibility, giving listeners the gift of what can be possible for their own lives.

1

I'm Oprah Winfrey. My purpose is to empower others to achieve their best lives. I enrich the lives of others by giving them the gifts of inspiration and fulfillment.

My name is Richard Branson and my purpose is to continually re-define what's possible through innovations, challenge endeavors, and charity efforts. I enrich the lives of others through innovative, cutting edge, technology-forward experiences. My contribution to the world is to not only define what's next but to do it.

I am Steve Jobs. And I believe that your time is wasted if you spend it living someone else's life. My brand purpose is to be unafraid to break the rules, to be part of technology's impact on the world, and be different. It is about innovation, technology, and the constant pursuit of excellence.

What do these innovative brand forces share as a common factor? They are all personal and dedicated to improving the world. Now more than ever, in a crowded marketplace, consumers want to know what exactly is your brand purpose? Why does your brand exist and how does it fit into their lives? And while we're at it, what can your brand deliver that no other can? How would you fill in this blank: My brand exists to _____. Whether you are an individual, entrepreneur, corporate executive, or brand marketer, you should be able to fill in that blank succinctly and meaningfully.

Why is your brand here? Consumers want to know and so does the world. Consumers are looking for brands that have a soul, and that soul is your brand purpose. As Scott Beaudoin, SVP/Global Director PurPle (Purpose + People) at MSLGROUP, said in the *New York Times*, "A lot of major, global companies are defining or redefining their purpose: what are they in the world to do? They're moving from marketing to serving the needs of consumers, figuring out ways to improve lives, better lives, while at the same time still be able to record profits on the corporate ledgers." He added that although "people understand the purpose of business is to make money, they are more skeptical than ever before about what brands and companies are doing. Profits being made with a greater purpose is what consumers are demanding."[1]

According to Beaudoin, purpose:

- Helps a brand stand for something.

- Provides the guiding light for innovation and opens up the door for deeper engagement.

- Provides a brand the opportunities to connect with authenticity, transparency, and meaning.

Let's look at what those terms mean.

- **Authenticity** helps you stand out and gives your brand a reason for being.

- **Transparency** allows customers to see into the soul, or essence, of your brand.

- **Meaning** connects emotionally with consumers; through meaning comes the chance to enrich the lives of others.

Now is the time to lead with purpose. Today offers a huge opportunity for marketers to bring forth great vision of how your brand can serve the world. In a recent interview with Bob Garfield on purpose-driven marketing, P&G former CMO Jim Stengel stressed that brands need to think in specific terms of better results, better performance, and more inspired people. It is *necessary* for your culture and your company to be empathetic, understanding, and service-oriented. From this higher purpose mindset, Pampers goes beyond selling diapers to becoming about baby development, or Tide goes beyond laundry detergent to becoming about helping mothers with their family's image. Above all, it's about getting people to experience your brand and become advocates. Think bigger, think higher, think about changing the world. The possibilities are endless when your brand leading with purpose.

As you ponder purpose, keep creativity at the heart and dream big. Creativity lies at the heart of marketing whether you are creating advertising, product positioning, consumer experiences, or messages. In some form or other you are always creating. With that in mind, challenge yourself each day to bring that sense of excitement, passion, wonder, imagination, and dreams to the table as part of your own creative process.

Truly great marketers dare to create the world they would like to see, not all at once but one idea, one activation, one engagement or campaign at a time. Over the past few years, I've been blessed with the opportunity of working alongside some of the great minds in marketing, many of whom served as teachers and mentors. What is the outstanding shared characteristic of these people? They dare to dream every single day. They approach each idea or campaign as an artist before a blank canvas and create what is possible. And that's what you must do: Consider each campaign as being dedicated to a higher purpose, one that will deliver good works to a world in need.

A Purposeful and Personal Journey

Before we go further, let me give you a glimpse of how my personal purpose-driven journey started. In often surprising and risky ways, I learned a great deal about thinking outside the box and dreaming big. Looking back over the past ten years of my own life, my start in multicultural marketing grew from one key element: a dream with a purpose. And, with every campaign or assignment, that same willingness to dare to dream has accompanied me. I know that this daring to dream is not just a helpful faculty but a required skill for every marketer. My own background provides substantial evidence. In 2002, I had a great job at IBM Global Services, working as Project Manager on one of its largest accounts, Best Buy in Minneapolis, Minnesota. At my yearly review I learned that my own manager had seen substantial growth in my work and was excited about my future at IBM. My review assessment scores were awesome. I was eligible for a significant pay raise. Why was I not ecstatic? Because I lacked passion for my career. Because of a small, inner voice that would not desist. It was telling me my destiny lay elsewhere.

Because my position at IBM was my first job straight out of college, it took me awhile to realize that career choices should be guided by more than just salary. Money was important to me. I got my first job in third grade when I convinced a dear friend of our family, Reverend Jones, to hire me to clean up an adult day care center five days a week and I managed to negotiate for a whopping $25 a week. That was followed by my job at thirteen as a waitress, followed by a number of jobs through high school and college. Suffice to say that the desire for money became the leading influencer in my career choice. Not until years later did I determine that you need to be passionate about your career, about the place in which you spend most of your time. Even though I'd learned a lot and received great training there, I gradually came to see that IBM was not for me. I was not only on the wrong side of the bus, I wasn't even on the correct bus, going in the right direction. Not until I was immersed in an MBA program did I finally have that explosive L-I-F-E bulb moment! The one that would put me on the right purpose-inspired career path and free me from spending time on a degree that didn't accommodate my dream.

It happened during one of my classes at the University of St. Thomas. I was assigned to write a life assessment paper, to write out all the reasons, choices, and influences that led me to pursue an MBA. My professor challenged us to think hard about what we wanted in our futures, about what was influencing those desires. The assignment, though difficult in its demands for soul searching, was in fact a great gift. Through it, I came to realize that all of my key life choices had been affected by earning potential—my Computer Science major in college, my job at IBM Global Services, with no regard to what I was truly passionate about. Now, in an MBA program, I was about to choose my entire future based on the same single factor, money, disregarding all other facets of my being.

This assignment was a gift, forcing me to open my mind and get honest with myself regarding who I truly was, and see that—contrary to what some might say about any ladle being sweet that dishes out the gravy—a career should be about more than just money; it must be an expression of your passion and gifts.

Now that I look back, I see that my personal purpose discovery journey also closely followed some basic principles of marketing. At the journey's start, I explored the number-one question a brand should explore and know: Why do you exist? I wanted to know that, and the best place to start was identifying what I had to authentically and uniquely give to others. So I started with the obvious, exploring my unique talents, skills, and values. I went through a process of assessing what I loved and what I naturally felt good at. If I were a product, I guess you could say I was determining my unique product attributes and benefits.

I was on a mission—but discovering my true passion was not a simple process. Far from it! I had to start by stepping back and looking into those aspects of life that I was naturally drawn to. I discovered that I love certain things:

- projects that allow me to express my creativity,

- working in environments that provide new projects and challenges on a daily basis,

- providing a platform with opportunities for emerging talent,

- pop culture: music and fashion,

- inspirational platforms that support me as well as others becoming better persons,

- connecting brands with multicultural audiences.

Above all, I discovered a love for the creative freedom and expression exemplified by urban culture's hip-hop movement. Throughout this book I'll cite both urban culture and hip-hop, so let's take a moment to clarify and define the terms. What's the difference? Well, urban culture (closely aligned to pop culture) refers to, rather than an actual geographic place, an attitude that identifies with hip-hop. For the ultimate definition of hip-hop, I turn to Russell Simmons. In his book *Life and Def: Sex, Drugs, Money, + God* (Crown, 2001) he says:

> To me, hip-hop is modern mainstream young urban American culture. I know there's a lot of ideas there, but hip-hop's impact is as broad as that description suggests. Like rock and roll, blues and jazz, hip-hop is primarily a musical form. But unlike those forms of black American music, hip-hop is more expansive in the

ways it manifests itself, and as a result, its impact is wider. The ideas of hip-hop are spread not just through music, but in fashion, movies, television advertising, dancing, slang and attitude. . . . I believe hip-hop is an attitude, one that can be nonverbal as well as eloquent. It communicates aspiration and frustration, community and aggression, creativity and street reality, style and substance. . . . Hip-hop has in fact changed the world. It has taken something from the American ghetto and made it global. It has become the creative touchstone for edgy, progressive and aggressive youth culture around the world.

An urban culture aficionado can live anywhere and is not confined to big cities. As for me, I was headed for the latter. The bright lights of New York were calling my name.

Russell Simmons' *Life and Def* really set me on fire and I found myself wondering how a country girl from the South could feel such a profound connection with urban culture's movement. While there were some elements that I viewed as controversial, did not agree with, and thought there was more room for growth, I was surprised to see that hip-hop and I had a great deal in common! We were both evolving and discovering our potential. The nickname "Tenacious Teneshia" more than complemented the thriving hip-hop culture—we shared an unrelenting inner drive. And, as I would later come to understand, brands that seek to emotionally connect with this fast-growing urban demographic would do well to deliver platforms that partner with them in the journey to success.

The hip-hop movement also reflected my own ability to dream big. What started as an underground movement had grown into a global phenomenon, the epitome of a dream realized. Often the artist's accomplishment of a certain level of success was expressed in the rhymes and lyrics. This aspirational language found its mate in my own strong desire to make it big one day. Later, I would come to know and understand the potential for luxury and high-end products to witness the power of the urban culture movement—the mention of your product in the right time and place can be the perfect endorser to spark word-of-mouth

(WOM) and trial. This once-niche market was now a key influencer of the mainstream, mirroring my desire to broaden my reach and have my creative gifts impact a greater audience. And who doesn't love the time-honored underdog who rises to the top? We all do, and brands that can build an emotional connection with consumers during their own evolution and rise are guaranteed to develop brand loyalty.

As Steve Stoute, author of *The Tanning of America: How Hip-Hop Created a Culture That Rewrote the Rules of the New Economy* (Gotham, 2011), so eloquently defines it, hip-hop is a:

> . . . catalytic *force majeure* that went beyond musical boundaries and into the psyche of young America—blurring cultural and demographic lines so permanently that it laid the foundation for a transformation that I have dubbed "tanning." Hip-hop had come about in a time, in places, and through multiple, innovative means that enabled it to level the playing field like no other movement of pop culture, allowing for a cultural exchange between all comers, groups of kids who were Black, White, Hispanic, Asian, you name it. Somehow this homegrown music resonated across racial and socio-economic lines and provided a cultural connection based on common experiences and values, and in turn it revealed a generationally shared mental complexion.

* * *

The milestone experience provided by *Life and Def* led me to become more excited about anything than I'd ever been before. While eagerly devouring Russell Simmons' vision of what the future had in store for the hip-hop movement, I was drawn to learning more about the man himself. There was an immediate attraction to this pioneer mind—a driving force that provided urban culture and hip-hop with a world stage.

Named by *USA Today* as one of the "Top 25 Most Influential People of the Past 25 Years," Russell Simmons' ground-breaking vision has profoundly influenced music, fashion, finance, television, and film, not to mention the state of contemporary philanthropy. Instrumental in bringing the powerful impact of hip-hop culture to virtually every aspect of business and media since its birth in the late 1970s, Simmons has been the master architect of that cultural phenomenon.

I imagined that Simmons had his defining purpose-inspired moment the night he first heard a new kind of music playing at Harlem's Charles' Gallery in 1977, especially "world-famous" Eddie Cheeba rhyming to excite the crowd. As Simmons writes in *Life and Def*, "Watching and hearing Cheeba had an equally powerful effect . . . and it hit me: I wanted to be in this business. Just like that I saw that I could turn my life in another, better way." From there, everything he touched (music, film, television, fashion) was grounded in his purpose to give life to hip-hop culture's creative expression.

Simmons has also noted several times that, accompanying his first moment of truth with hip-hop sound, was a burning desire to share it with the world. In common with all great minds, he also desired to provide value to others. It wasn't just about what he could make for himself. He was on a mission with a higher purpose. His desire was first and foremost to give a great sound to the world. He wanted to enrich the lives of others, not just in New York, not just in the U.S., but also throughout the entire world. And did he ever meet demand! Consumers globally would connect with this movement, leading to a billion-dollar enterprise comprising fashion, media, finance, music, technology. There is hardly a category untouched by the power of this culture.

So you can clearly see why reading this man's story was monumental for me; why it provided a defining moment in my journey of self-discovery. After reading Simmons' book, I was determined to carve out a place to contribute to and participate in the urban movement. Analyzing the key influential people within urban culture, I looked at how and where they got their start. The backgrounds of people like P. Diddy, Kevin Liles, Julie Greenwald, and Lyhor Cohen shared a common factor—a willingness to jump in and start giving, regardless of financial gain. All had a dream with a purpose, grounded in a desire to serve. This exemplifies servant-style leadership that has become relevant again in this economic environment. As Larry Julian says in his book *God Is My CEO* (Adams Media, 2002), "Those of us who are leaders of an organization should work to create a mission in which our organization's purpose is more than just making money." A leader must be one who serves, not uses, others.

With these examples before me, I started to think in a new direction. I wondered, how many people would refuse a person (with my professional background) who offered to work for them for no fee? Just for the opportunity to learn. I wanted to co-create and add value to this movement and in return I would receive value and knowledge. I felt certain that most people would welcome such a worker. I felt certain that there was a reserved seat at the urban culture table with my name on it. As a creative marketer, I can't stress enough how crucial it is to bring the power of imagination and belief to the table. This type of belief in imagination might appear radical—but did you know that Webster's defines genius as "extraordinary intellectual power especially as manifested in creative activity?" By those lights, radical doesn't take it far enough! Nineteenth-century German philosopher Arthur Schopenhauer was even more concise: "Talent hits a target no one else can hit. Genius hits a target no one else can see."

Finally, I reached the point where I knew I'd enter a new field. This meant departing from IBM at the height of my career there, having received the best review of my professional life. Crazy? Some might have thought so, but I was ready to follow my heart and try for that target no one else could see. Trusting my gut instinct this way took every ounce of courage I had, but I did it. A gut instinct after all, beats all the learning in the world because it cannot be taught. Think about your role as marketer and gut instincts. How many times have you experienced one, how often did you have the courage to follow up on it?

Trusting *my* gut instinct meant taking a huge leap of faith, bidding farewell to a secure job, and setting off to find the door that would open for me in hip-hop—an extraordinary industry, with a consumer demographic that had its finger on the pulse of everything from music, fashion, arts, finance, fast food, sports, technology, and more. The buying power of this demographic grows at a ferocious rate. *Packaged Facts* projects that "the aggregate income of Young Urban Consumers will grow from $594 billion in 2007 to $684 billion in 2012. This represents cumulative growth of 15 percent. The age segment registering the largest rate of growth will be 25-to-34-year-olds. The aggregate income of Young Urban Consumers in this age bracket will increase by 17 percent, from $402 billion to $468 billion. Aggregate income of teen Young Urban Consumers is projected to increase from $42 billion to $45 billion, an increase of seven percent. The aggregate income of college age (18 to 24) Young Urban Consumers is expected to grown from $151 billion to $171 billion, representing cumulative growth of 14 percent."[2]

A Plan to Break into Hip-Hop

Getting back to my dream journey, I was determined to break into hip-hop and started strategizing a plan. I began to frequent particular key events that presented networking opportunities. Fortuitously, shortly after reading his book, I encountered Russell Simmons at the Fashion Magic Show in Las Vegas. Stepping up to the plate, I shared with him my dream of working with his organization and offered to "shadow" him and learn the business of urban culture, sans salary. After a few more admittedly not-so-accidental encounters with Russell, I continued to press my case, offering him my services in exchange for a chance to learn. I went to New York and requested a meeting with the great Mr. Simmons. When the answer was no, I moved to New York so that I could persist in my follow up. And when I say persist, you can read maniacal! At last, after 30 faxed letters, and standing up in front of a crowd where he was speaking and asking him point blank, "What do you have to lose? Why not give it a try . . ." Well, let's say even Simmons became curious at this point. Crazy or genius? That's how I took cold call to the next level.

Finally, he took me up on my offer and invited me to his office to start shadowing both him and his executive team. During those first few exciting months, I began to see firsthand the power of urban culture and how it was impacting many business categories. RUSH Communications is a top holding company with multi-faceted investments in important brands in three industry segments: entertainment and media; fashion and lifestyle; and empowerment. Among the many brands were:

- Phat Fashions, a clothing line, and lifestyle fashion and jewelry lines American Classics, Argyle Culture, Pastry, Run Athletics, and Simmons Jewelry;

- RUSH card, a financial services company;

- DefCon 3, the energy drink;

- Def Jam Enterprises, a gaming division;

- RUSH Community Affairs, a philanthropic division made up of a number of philanthropic non-profits serving multicultural communities;

- RUSH Philanthropic Arts Foundation, dedicated to providing disadvantaged urban youth with significant exposure and access to the arts, and to offering exhibition opportunities for under-represented artists and artists of color;

- Diamond Empowerment Fund, a non-profit international organization with the mission to raise money to support education initiatives that develop and empower economically disadvantaged people in African nations where diamonds are a natural resource;

- Hip-Hop Summit Action Network (HSAN), dedicated to harnessing the cultural relevance of Hip-Hop music to serve as a catalyst for education advocacy and other societal concerns fundamental to the empowerment of youth;

- Foundation of Ethnic Understanding, committed to the belief that direct, face-to-face dialogue between ethnic communities is the most effective path towards the reduction of bigotry and the promotion of reconciliation and understanding; and

- Global Grind, a community-based site that allows users to discover, collect and share the most relevant web content for the hip-hop community in the U.S. and internationally.

As you can see, Russell's RUSH Communications empire spanned many business categories including a division dedicated to giving back.

The offices overflowed with young creative talent of all races, in a laid-back environment conducive to entrepreneurship. If you worked hard, it was noticed. There was no corporate career track that had to be adhered to. People like Kevin Liles had gone from intern to president of Def Jam within eight years. The only law of the land was that in hip-hop anything was possible. They not only knew the urban consumer inside out, the very fabric of the company reflected it.

Often, as marketers, we are up to our ears in market research just to meet our customers; not so for Simmons and his entrepreneurial brilliance. For him, it wasn't about the research, but staying close to his consumer and making an effort to build an office culture that reflected the diversity of urban consumers, by immersing himself in their world. The global hip-hop community includes about 24 million people aged 19 to 34, from a range of nationalities, ethnic groups, and religions. Their collective spending power is $500 billion annually in the U.S. alone.[3] Simmons made sure the office reflected the diversity and demographic make-up of the culture.

Simmons had a vision and he could also anticipate the next needs of the culture. For example, just by being close to the consumer, he recognized that a significant portion of them did not have access to debit or credit cards. Simmons immediately spotted a need and responded to it automatically, no market research necessary. Take a look at the launch of what came to be the RUSH card, a prepaid VISA card. From its inception, the product had a unique purpose, and it was about far more than the financial industry. It was about empowering citizens of the urban culture with choices that were previously denied them, and seizing an opportunity. While the RUSH card was not without some negative reviews and controversy, and Simmons' way of advocating for financial empowerment has been questioned, the objective was grounded in a need to provide these consumers with an experience that they had been denied.

During those days, my function was akin to that of a sponge in such a vibrantly creative environment. My goal was to absorb as much as I possibly could and learn everything about it. It didn't take long to realize I was among the "Who's Next" great minds of urban culture. There was Myorr Jahna, leading the growth of Phat Fashions, a company that later sold to Kellwood for $140 million dollars. Myorr rose from front-desk receptionist to vice-president within three years. Leading fashion trends for urban and mainstream culture, he was the influencer's influencer. There was also Kevin Leong, a young Asian-American kid with a gift for fashion design. No Fashion Institute of Technology grad, Kevin had pitched himself in a short elevator ride and worked his way up to Phat Fashions' lead designer. Then there was Ellen Haddigan, a conservative-looking white lady in her mid-40s who was rolling with Simmons everywhere. I wondered what such an unlikely person was doing in a hip-hop office and would later learn that, although not the typical consumer demographic, Ellen played a critical role in connecting with hip-hop purpose in serving as a catalyst and advocate for change, leading RUSH Community Affairs, Simmons' philanthropic division.

A Higher Purpose for Hip-Hop

As one of the founding godfathers, it doesn't surprise me even remotely that Simmons was among the first hip-hop leaders to explore a higher purpose for the movement. Could such a movement have a higher purpose? Could it be a powerful vehicle to affect change, to address social issues facing our community and impact global causes? The answer, we now know, is a resounding yes. Simmons had an intuitive hunch that his urban culture consumers were ready to serve as agents of change. He knew that introducing socially responsible platforms and engagements would resonate with this audience. In fact, we later found that 87 percent of urban consumers identify with the notion of taking responsibility. In this process, I believe we were shaping a new cool reality—an element of cool that now included purpose.

As I look back now, I can see that serendipitously I was aligning to my own purpose; I was about to be given opportunities to deliver purpose-inspired engagement to urban culture. One day, I was sitting at the desk of Simmons' vice president, Gary Foster. Simmons had asked Gary to mentor me and let me share his office. So there I was—a young lady who had literally dreamed her way into this company and suddenly this executive finds himself sharing his office with an intern! In some corporate environments, that would not have gone over too well. But Simmons had cultivated such an amazing environment that had servant-style leadership woven into its fabric that this VP welcomed me into his office.

It's interesting at this point to take a step back and see that consumers equate "leading company" with being "innovative" and "ethical." Consumers expect purpose to start within and to be woven into the employee workforce, too. "Incorporating consumers into the development and execution phases of the cause initiative enhances the authenticity of the program, while also boosting company morale and consumer loyalty."[4] It's a fact. Consumers look to your internal company make-up, to your employees to determine what type of company you are. Simmons built a company that reflected his values from within; this was evident by a senior level executive, Gary, who personified the spirit of that company and was willing to teach an intern.

For myself, let's just say I learned firsthand the power of being willing to work hard and (as Simmons would say) keep my head down. Some of my early assignments certainly taught me humility. When a former IBM executive finds herself cleaning offices and organizing files, there's nothing else to call it! I could have shunned the idea, but that cleaning assignment was the best thing that could have happened. It gave me the opportunity to read every business contract and see the wide range of deals that were on the table, from Motorola-branded phones to new perfume lines with Coty, to IMG Fashion Week Opening night opportunities for Baby Phat, to energy drinks DefCon 3, and more. In those early days I was a sponge and, though an unusual orientation, it provided me with a priceless overview of the power of the hip-hop market.

Another time, I was sitting in Foster's office when Simmons came in and blew a fuse. He was upset because a pet project of his was hitting the dust. This project, The Hip-Hop Reader, was a literacy initiative aimed at increasing reading rates in New York City schools. He thought that urban culture could serve as a catalyst that would make reading "cool" for students. Fortunately for me, the project was crumbling. Now, after sitting quietly for three months, the time had come for me to speak up and seize the opportunity. As Eminem so memorably expressed it,

Look, if you had one shot, or one opportunity
To seize everything you ever wanted in one moment
Would you capture it or just let it slip?
You better lose yourself in the music, the moment,
You own it, you better never let it go,
You only get one shot, do not miss your chance to blow,
This opportunity comes once in a lifetime, yo!
                    —Eminem, "One Shot–Lose Yourself"

So I spoke up nervously, "Russell, give me the project. I can do this—I bring more than enough project management skills to the table to support it." For a moment he was shocked that the quiet one (me) had spoken up so forcefully. Then, true to form for a man of brilliant intuition, he said, "Gary, give her the project. It's so f**** up that we have nothing to lose." And in that instant I was off and running with

my first purpose-inspired project in hip-hop.

The Hip-Hop Reader initiative was funded by the Verizon Foundation through a partnership between National Urban League and Hip-Hop Summit Action Network. With a mission to make reading more appealing to young students, we had to connect with youngsters through their interest in urban culture and fashion.

Reading for Rewards

Essentially, the project was something like an educational reading rewards program. Students could earn points for their required reading assignments. The program featured an online interactive site that allowed students to share during reading and engage with their peers. It also paralleled some of the school's reading assignments with modern lyrics. This translation made the students' reading assignments relevant to urban culture within the classroom and connected students with their language. Influential hip-hop lyrical artists shared their favorite books to create a reading list for each student grade level.

Why would students care about earning points? Because the points had power! They could be used to redeem the latest urban culture fashions, which, at the time, included Rockawear, Sean John, Baby Phat, Def Jam music, and so on. The goal was to have reading become "cool" and have New York City schools adopt the program. But why would Verizon care about having a brand presence with this program?

Verizon cared about having a brand presence with this program because, for years, it had prioritized the multicultural community and this program was an example of that priority. Verizon understood the importance and the consumer expectation of having brands show up in the community. Traditionally, expectations run low among African Americans for the commitment of brands to their community. While 83 percent agree that companies that make a sincere effort to be a part of the African-American community deserve their loyalty, 67 percent say, "Because businesses are too concerned about offending the general population, they fail to take a firm stand on issues that are important to minorities."

This project called urgently on all of my IBM project-management experience. Obtaining an understanding of all parties involved was key. They were Verizon Wireless Foundation, a brand that was able to support community with leading social issue education, and The National Urban League that brought its own impeccable credibility as a long-standing community partner in the African-American community with a mission to empower. Finally, the Hip-Hop Summit Action Network, Simmons' recently launched non-profit, was the largest coalition of artists founded on the belief that hip-hop as a movement could be a catalyst for change and empowerment.

Through the meetings with labels—from Def Jam (Lauren Wirtzer) agreeing to donate the latest CDs from leading music artists as prizes, to the leading fashion brands Rockawear, Sean Jean, and Enyce agreeing to donate gear as prizes—I grew to understand that everyone was passionate to help and support and above all to *use* the power of hip-hop as inspiration. Just possibly Simmons was on to something. Perhaps this catalytic force would become a huge driver of empowerment. I was *soooo* nervous about the launch of this project! It was held in Harlem at the historic Schomberg Center, a perfect opportunity to use a heritage site that resonates with the community.

On the day itself, my mom flew into town to lend support for my project debut. Thanks, Mama, it meant the world! *(Shout out to my mom—Carolyn Hearns . . . smile.)* I think she had to see for herself what had led her daughter to leave corporate IBM and work for no fee.

The pressure was on. Not only did I want the project to succeed, I think I also wanted her to see that the passion move was going to pay off. So what happened?

The launch of the program was a huge success! Ultimately, over 1,000 young people attended the event, with nationwide coverage including a segment on BET's *106th & Park,* television's number one video countdown show.

This early assignment demonstrated the power of hip-hop to inspire young students while also connecting products and brands to a cause that was important to the community. Russell Simmons, Drew Barrymore, Damon Dash, Jim Jones, Fonzworth Bentley, Rev. Run, and Camron were among the celebrity supporters who attended the launch event and shared their own favorite books with students.

HIP-HOP READER LAUNCH EVENT

TOP
Fonzworth Bentley and Russell Simmons.

BOTTOM
Kevin Liles (former president of Def Jam, Warner music executive) and Luv Bug Starski (American MC)

These were not paid appearances; they came out of a desire to leverage celebrity to do something meaningful. As will be discussed later, there is great value in providing celebrities with a platform to do good works. Not only was it ground-breaking in driving reading interest among multicultural students, the project was adopted by 20 New York City schools, dramatically proving the power of hip-hop to inspire educational platforms. This is a prime example of some of the early urban culture's purpose-driven marketing at work.

TAKEAWAYS

1. **Why is your brand here?** Consumers want to know and so does the world. Consumers are looking for brands that have a soul and that soul is your brand purpose.

2. As you ponder purpose, **keep creativity at the heart and dream big.** Creativity lies at the heart of marketing whether you are creating advertising, product positioning, consumer experiences, or messages. In some form or other you are always creating. With that in mind, challenge yourself each day to bring that sense of excitement, passion, wonder, imagination, and dreams to the table as part of your own creative process.

3. **Seize the moment**; there is no time like NOW to deliver your brand purpose to the world.

Notes

1. *The New York Times* July 15, 2011.
2. The Young Urban Consumer Market in the U.S.: How Hip-Hop Culture Affects the Lifestyle and Buying Decisions of 12- to 34-Year Olds, 3rd Edition, May 2008.
3. audiblehype.com
4. Urban Influencer Panel Series 2011.

Chapter 2

Define Your Brand Purpose

Where your talents and the needs of the world cross, there lies your purpose.

—Aristotle

As EVERYONE in the universe knows, Oprah Winfrey ended her amazing talk show in 2011. Now proprietor of the OWN network, two of her top shows are two of my favorites: *Master Class* and *Life Class.* Saying that I am a fan is an understatement in view of the sweaty palms and accelerated heartbeat that characterize my viewing posture. Before you start wondering how this is relevant to marketing, bear with me.

First, Oprah has always championed finding your purpose in life, whoever you are. And, as far as your brand goes, this advice is a perfect fit. Think about it. A lot of brands out there are still trying to determine what their purpose is. I think Oprah has many valuable lessons to offer the world of marketing. After all, she's not only achieved her own purpose, she's also created a phenomenal brand at the same time. According to Oprah, "Purpose feels like the right space for you, like what you SHOULD be doing." For brands, it's the ownable unique space that only you can deliver to your customers and the world.

Once your brand purpose is identified, you'll be home. If you're in the dark as to how to locate this purpose, try looking backwards, to the founding roots of your company. What ideas were behind its beginnings and what did its creators believe in? Shine a light in that attic and you're likely to strike gold. Also, listen to what your fans are saying about you. It could be that they have perspectives that have passed you by. Most importantly, be yourself. No one believes a faker—so why waste your time trying to be something you're not? As Oprah says, be your authentic self. If you're unsure about who or what that is, your immediate goal is to find out.

After watching Oprah's purpose episode of *Life Class,* I absolutely believe marketers can take a page out of her purpose manual. Now that we've set the stage of why purpose is important through the eyes of Oprah, let's discuss what the marketing industry thinks of purpose.

Brand is defined by the American Marketing Association as the "name, term, design, symbol, or any other feature that identifies one seller's good or service as distinct from those of all other sellers." Sounds pretty simple. But what about promise, and even more importantly— what about purpose? To thrive today, it is necessary to define your brand's purpose as well as its promise. Merely being able to remember a brand's name is insignificant to brand equity if consumers don't understand what the brand can actually do for them and above all, why it matters. Strong brands become that way when people know not only what the brands stand for, but also how they fit into their lives.

Some Essential Steps to Uncover Your Brand Purpose

Our own purpose expert, MS&L Group's Global Director of Purpose, Scott Beaudoin, states, "Brands over the years have struggled to align on the societal issues, to really help not only differentiate the brand, to give it a halo, and the missing link over the years has been purpose." Purpose is not a new concept—think of Rick Warren's mega best-seller *The Purpose Driven Life* (Zondervan, 2002). Certainly, purpose is key to the meaning of life. Taking a page out of Oprah's purpose manual, life can sometimes feel meaningless without a purpose. Brands, like people, must also have a reason for existence. Consumers and other stakeholders are definitely looking for brands to have a soul. And that soul which is being defined today is really a guiding light to how the brand innovates in ways that are helping people every day through core competencies, i.e., what a brand can really deliver that no other brand can deliver.

How to Unlock Your Brand's Purpose

With that in mind, let's talk about the essential steps to unlocking your brand purpose. In my opinion, Procter & Gamble is leading this, and it always starts at the top of the food chain. A leading Global Marketing Officer (P&G's Marc Pritchard) has given speeches on this topic at the Association of National Advertisers (ANA) "Masters of Marketing" conference. A former GMO, Jim Stengel, has written a must-read book called *Grow: How Ideals Power Growth and Profit at the World's Greatest Companies* (Crown Business, 2011). When CEOs are concerned about purpose, you can bet it trickles down so that it almost becomes mandatory.

However, there's no specific set way of unlocking what the purpose is. As Scott Beaudoin says, some brands like P&G are doing it really, *really* well, while others? Not so much. Many companies are still stuck on the idea of product benefits, which often creates purpose statements that are narrow and challenging to leverage as a way to engage. Cause marketers, on the other hand, have been doing this kind of work for many years.

Our question is, what is it the brand provides the consumer that is more over-arching as a benefit, emotionally and socially, requiring the brand to think a bit bigger, and be more aspirational? Let's take the leading toothpaste, Crest, for example. It makes you more confident in your mouth, the place where everything starts. If you're confident about your oral health, you open up more. If you open up more, what does that do for you? You open up to world, the world opens up to you, and good things happen. Hence the purpose of oral care is to help people engage in the world more confidently, period.

This process requires the brand to think through some things. What is the brand delivering on? Due to your product's existence in the consumer's life, what becomes possible for the consumer? This describes our process in developing purpose-inspired programs that are grounded in what the brand is all about.

In another recent example, Roy M. Spence, Jr., co-author of *It's Not What You Sell, It's What You Stand For: Why Every Extraordinary Business*

Is Driven by Purpose (Portfolio, 2009) talked about purpose in a B2B online magazine interview. Spence cited several purpose-inspired clients of his agency, including Motorola Solutions and Southwest Airlines. In Motorola's case, the purpose is succinctly stated: "We help people be the best they can be in the moments that matter most," while Southwest's purpose is captured in its slogan: "We give people the freedom to fly." Stating that this was borne out in the carrier's response to competitors' decisions to charge for checked bags, Spence pointed out that Southwest decided to pass up this additional revenue stream because it flew in the face of the airline's purpose. Instead, it launched its "Bags Fly Free" campaign—a move that ended up paying off handsomely, as the decision not to charge for checked bags resulted in $1.2 billion in new revenue.[1]

For more brands whose ideals have paid off handsomely, take a look at Jim Stengel's book *Grow*. He and his team invented ideals statements for companies like Accenture ("Accenture exists to help people accelerate ideas to achieve their dreams"), Amazon.com ("Amazon.com exists to enable freedom of choice, exploration and discovery"), Pampers ("Pampers exists to help mothers care for their babies' and toddlers' healthy, happy development"), and Red Bull ("Red Bull exists to energize the world"). Get the picture?

When it comes to brands that clearly define their purpose and deliver purpose engagements to multicultural audiences, I have some favorites that you'll learn about throughout this book. Just as brands must explore their higher meaning, I also was on a journey to find my personal meaning and I think this is the perfect time to share with you a little more of my own journey and take you through the process that I followed in defining my personal brand purpose.

The Journey Continues

After the Hip-Hop Reader Project, I was on a high and knew I'd definitely entered my personal purpose zone. Shortly afterwards, I had the opportunity to work directly with Russell Simmons. Instead of going on payroll as an employee, which conflicted with my vision of going

down an entrepreneur path, I negotiated that Simmons would retain
my company for the work I provided. One problem: I didn't have a
company yet! Thus, I quickly formed a business structure, Egami Group,
and Simmons became my first client. While I didn't have a clear idea
how the company would grow or what it would ultimately become, it
would at least provide project management and organization services to
RUSH Communications. The year was 2003; I was 26.

Even though I was working for my own business, I was on site daily
at the RUSH office for the next four years and very much a part of
Simmons' day-to-day team. Originally, I served as project manager to
a number of projects, such as Hip-Hop Summit Action Network/Get
Out the Vote Campaign, Get Ya Money Right, Get Your Home Right,
and so on. Within a year, I went from intern to being named General
Manager of Russell's RUSH Communications. In that capacity I was
responsible for organization development and day-to-day operations.
If I had to sum up that role, I like to say that I felt responsible for
infusing a bit of "corporate structure" into the creative offices built on
hip-hop. As I continued to strive to define my personal brand purpose,
I continued to ask questions:

- Am I adding value to others and my clients?

- Am I leveraging all of my skill sets and assets to uniquely serve
  others and meet a need?

- How can I provide greater value?

Constantly thinking about how to add value to others with your
special talents and products will help you understand and define your
brand purpose. As Scott Beaudoin describes it, explore the brand's process to discover its emotional meaning in consumers' lives.

For example, if I provide X, what then becomes possible for the
consumer? In my case, by providing the industry with knowledge of
Corporate America, what became possible? During this process, I realized
I wasn't fully leveraging my experience in Corporate America. I knew I'd
left it behind to completely immerse myself in a creative entertainment
environment but the truth of the matter is that I was still corporate.

That meant I was the only one in the RUSH office constantly pushing for a new "process" or a new "procedure." This creative company did not have a process manual lying around but I was always asking for it. However, true to hip-hop culture, if you wanted to see it done, you did it yourself, which led to my writing a lot of the process and procedures for RUSH Communications over the next couple of years.

The corporate life that I'd fled was now part of the value I added to hip-hop and urban culture. It became clear that my time at IBM was not wasted. It was part of my journey and gave me the ability to carve out a unique spot within RUSH. Sometimes on our personal purpose journey, it can be frustrating if you feel you are far from your purpose. I encourage you to be patient in those moments. As I've learned, even those experiences can support you in bringing your purpose to life. Thus I started to ask myself some questions. *Given that my previous "corporate" experience seemed to be serving a niche within an urban culture environment such as RUSH, how could I further leverage my corporate experience while remaining close to urban culture and entertainment?* No doubt you're familiar with the old saying that when the student is ready the teacher appears. My teacher appeared as an opportunity to work on a project that would teach me that there was indeed a need at the intersection of Corporate and Hip-Hop. L-I-F-E Bulb Moment: My love of both could work!

Capturing Memories

Jostens, a leading provider of special gifts for U.S. high school students, asked me to work with its marketing team on rolling out an urban product line. So Jostens was my teacher and here's why: Its purpose is inherently in capturing cherished memories. However, one of the key essentials is also understanding your consumer. Was it capturing memories in ways that were relevant to *its* consumers? Curious to see if it should market or at least take a look at the urban consumer, I took the opportunity to provide strategic marketing counsel to the senior marketing team. It was with this project that I realized many corporate brands had a lot to learn when it comes to the urban market. In this case, the first thing was understanding the target. Using the experience I'd gained working at RUSH, here's what I was able to share with Jostens:

- Urban mindset is not a geographical place: Nearly four in ten (39 percent) of urban lifestyle consumers live in suburban areas.

- Their collective spending power is $644 billion annually in the U.S. alone.

- Urban consumers are multi-racial: The global hip-hop community comprises 24 million people aged 19 to 34, from a range of nationalities, ethnic groups, and religions.

- Racial background majority is White, followed by Hispanic, followed by Black.

Indeed, in addition to *not* being a geographical place, urban culture was not a niche market. One out of two high school students identified with the culture. So, Jostens could ill afford to ignore this mindset and instead, sought to better connect with it. Other important aspects we knew about these consumers were their:

- **Love of fashion:** Each month urban consumers spend 45 percent more on clothing, accessories, and shoes than non-urban consumers.

- **Love of music:** Urban consumers spend close to $9 billion yearly on recreational and entertainment activities.

- **Trusted sources in their influencers:** Celebrities pack a wallop when it comes to influencing fans in all areas of their lives.

After these and more demographic studies were examined, Jostens launched the first-ever urban graduate product line. By understanding these consumers, Jostens found the perfect way to connect with their love of fashion and style, and give them culturally relevant products that supported them in capturing memories while recognizing the influence of celebrities in their lifestyle. Serving as the connector, the project provided me (along with my team) the opportunity to provide counsel. It also enabled us to leverage existing urban culture relationships built over the last few years, bringing those relationships new and exciting project opportunities in which to participate.

I can remember pitching Kimora Simmons' team on the idea of the KLS brand providing products to support teens celebrating the milestone of graduation. They immediately thought it was a perfect new opportunity and yet another way to impact urban culture. Jostens' urban graduate product line included the Class of 2008 House of Dereon Beyoncé class ring, Class of 2008 Baby Phat hoodie, and more. For over two years, the House of Dereon Beyoncé class ring was a leading seller.

The Jostens' project was another big L-I-F-E Bulb moment for me. After that experience, I knew I wanted to continue to act as a connector between corporate brands, urban and multicultural consumers, and communities. It felt right, like part of my purpose, and exactly like what I was supposed to be doing at that point in my life.

Strangely enough, during this time a dear friend and colleague, Donnell Byrd, who was currently serving as VP of RUSH Card, reviewed the work I was doing at Jostens and said, "T, you are an agency!" Full disclosure: My response was, "Donnell, an agency? What type of services does an agency provide its clients?" Although I did not have the corporate structure of an agency or even the language to describe my services, I was being true and authentic to my purpose. As a result, I was delivering multicultural marketing and public relations work that was results driven. What Jostens got was an innovative, creative, culturally relevant urban marketing strategy that delivered business RESULTS. My lack of an agency background was insignificant. When you are purpose driven, anything is possible.

I now understood what I'd heard Russell Simmons say years before. While talking about Kevin Liles (former president of Def Jam), he mentioned that Liles was president of Def Jam long before he received the title. For you readers who are also on a path of defining your personal brand, remember this: you don't need a title to start being purpose driven. Your number one priority is to stay true to your unique characteristics. In my case, when I was purpose driven, my brand purpose was born.

Egami Consulting Group officially became a full-service multicultural marketing firm connecting corporate brands to urban/multicultural audiences. The firm continued to work with Simmons and other corporate brands such as Jostens. A few years later, I was introduced to the MSLGROUP, a leading consumer engagement firm which is part of Publicis Groupe, one of the world's three largest advertising holding companies. MSLGROUP was an industry leader in engagement and had an extensive client roster. Its executive agency team had a vision and could see the power of growing multicultural markets. In order for their firm to continue to deliver client solutions reflective of American demographics, they desired to provide clients with diversity solutions. Forming a strategic alliance, Egami Consulting Group became the diversity marketing partner to the firm. I'm grateful to the MSL Group executive team, that has been supportive of our five-year, award winning diversity partnership.

TAKEAWAYS

1. **Once your brand purpose is identified, you'll be home**. If you're in the dark as to how to locate this purpose, try looking backwards to the founding roots of your company. What ideas were behind its beginnings and what did its creators believe in? Shine a light in that attic and you're likely to strike gold.

2. To thrive today, it is necessary to **define your brand's purpose as well as its promise.** Merely being able to remember a brand's name is insignificant to brand equity if consumers don't understand what the brand can actually do for them and above all, why it matters. Strong brands become that way when people know not only what the brand stands for, but also how it fits into their lives.

3. **By *understanding* urban consumers,** you can find the perfect way to connect with their love of fashion, music and style, to deliver culturally relevant products and programs to this demographic.

4. As you think of bringing your brand purpose to life, ask yourself "What is it my brand can provide my consumer that is **more over-arching as a benefit, emotionally and socially,** and requires my brand to think a bit bigger and to be more aspirational."

Note

1. www.btobonline.com/article/20110602/STRATEGY02/306029992/bma-annual-purpose-inspired-marketing-crucial-to-winning-business#seenit)

Chapter 3

Two Brands That Have Successfully Defined Purpose

HERE ARE TWO GREAT EXAMPLES of brands delivering purpose-inspired work to multicultural communities, which MSL Group and Egami have been privileged to work on.

The Bounty "Messterpiece" campaign

The challenge was to launch an experiential youth arts marketing effort led by P&G's Bounty® paper towel brand, promoting its purpose of being "hands on." Bounty had a unique opportunity to provide youth with "hands on" creative experiences to foster learning. Knowing that children are a part of what matters most to the Bounty Mom, this program provided the perfect opportunity to connect with its target in a meaningful and purposeful way. The *promise* was to unlock children's creativity and improve academic performance through the vital link between creativity and critical thinking. So what happened?

To begin with, public survey data found a low priority on school art funding. While arts programming and creativity were needed, they were losing a platform within American schools and communities. Taking this a step further, we looked at Bounty's desire to connect with multicultural communities and found there was a definite need due to lack of arts education within multicultural communities, while at the same time, a Harris Poll revealed that 93 percent of Americans believe that the arts are vital to providing a well-rounded education.[1] Based on my work with

Russell Simmons, I knew of his ten-year track record of delivering arts programs to children within underserved multicultural communities via his non-profit RUSH Arts Foundations. Locating a community partner that aligns with your brand purpose is a great way to deliver purposeful programs within multicultural communities. Eighty-nine percent of African Americans and 90 percent of Hispanics agree, "companies that make sincere efforts to be part of the African-American/Hispanic community deserve my loyalty."[2]

Given these insights, Bounty partnered with Russell Simmons' RUSH Philanthropic Arts Foundation youth groups and teaching artists to conduct a six-city (New York, Chicago, San Francisco, Washington, D.C., New Orleans, and Cincinnati) arts tour—*Building Bounty-ful Bridges*—that traversed the United States encouraging kids to be hands-on and learn by doing (the basis of Bounty brand purpose). Further, Bounty leveraged RUSH Philanthropic's connections to key influencers and endorsers—garnering support from advocating celebrities that joined us and made appearances at the national launch and unveiling events. The celebrities included Mary J. Blige, Susan Sarandon, Ana Ortiz, fashion designer Tory Burch, and Joseph "Rev. Run" Simmons. Kids in the six cities, under the creative direction of RUSH Philanthropic Director of Education, Meredith McNeal and featured artist Amanda Williams, were engaged in the "Building Bounty-ful Bridges" program—a large scale collaborative painting that "bridged" them creatively with others across the country.

The result of this unparalleled nationwide collaboration was exhibited at New York's RUSH Arts Gallery, a space providing exhibition opportunities to an emerging artistic community and exposing disadvantaged urban youth to contemporary arts and culture through educational programming initiatives. And, at a time when many schools have had to make painful decisions about cutting programs, Bounty was proud to support hands-on learning through the arts.

"At Bounty, we saw the Make-a-Messterpiece studio, along with the RUSH Philanthropic Arts Foundation partnership as opportunities to help children grow and learn by sponsoring fun, 'hands-on' activities that encourage curiosity and creativity outside the classroom," said Eric

Higgs, brand manager for Bounty. "It is our way of saying 'never let messes get in the way of your children learning and trying new things.'" Russell Simmons added, "I'm excited that RUSH Philanthropic is partnering with Bounty to help promote artistic expression among youth in communities all across the country . . . Bounty is providing a much-needed space for local children to realize their creative potential." This is more than just talk. A Stanford University study found that youngsters who participate in the arts are four times more likely to be recognized for academic achievement.

That adage we were all raised with, "don't make a mess," went out the window with the innovative Make-a-Messterpiece campaign. MAM broadened beyond the traditional marketing boundaries and really engaged consumers in a fresh (and interactive) way. Activities at the Messterpiece Studio include:

- *Kids Creative Kitchen:* using science and math concepts to make tasty treats;
- *Bubble'ology:* using air movement to teach cause and effect;
- *Little Sprouts:* getting kids involved with nature—fostering responsibility and nurturing;
- *Drum Roll:* focusing on rhythm and sequence, fundamental math skills;
- *Experimentation Station:* a rotating science station where kids learn creative problem-solving skills.

From left: Russell Simmons, Mary J. Blige and Bounty Associated Brand Manager, Chris Brown

Within structured, supervised play and learning activities, children can make as big a mess as they please using all kinds of media including crayons, paint, markers, construction paper, glitter, glue, and musical instruments. Trained staff interact with the kids in an endlessly creative and open environment and, at day's end, proud parents get to enjoy their children's "Messterpieces."

In the end, the campaign triumphed, reaping more than 650MM impressions nationwide through an exclusive with Reuters and top placements on VH1's *Celebrities Gone Good* and WNBC-TV's *Talk Stoop,* Starmagazine.com, *Chicago Tribune* mommy blog, *Time Out Chicago Kids,* and the *New York Daily News.*

This is purpose-driven marketing at work. Or, as creative director Simon Mainwaring calls it in his book of the same name, "We First" marketing. "Corporations need to allow consumers to co-create their brands, invite consumers to help them with causes, build social capital with consumers, and reach out to consumers allowing them to vote for the brand every day." In this case Bounty allowed the multicultural communities to co-create and participate in its "hands on" purpose via this nationwide arts experience.

From the color of my skin, to the texture of my hair, to the length of my strands, to the breadth of my smile... *My Black is Beautiful.*

JOIN THE MOVEMENT & CELEBRATE YOUR UNIQUE BEAUTY

My Black is Beautiful

Another solid example of a brand offering both promise and purpose is P&G's *My Black is Beautiful* (MBIB) campaign. As an African-American woman, I freely admit that working on this account is like waking up Christmas morning to the best present ever. MBIB's brand purpose is "We exist to help give voice to Black women in expressing their true and best self to the world." Its mission is "To inspire a dialogue among African-American women to define their own standards, and to affirm and celebrate the individual and collective beauty of African-American women." The movement resonates powerfully with Black women across the nation, giving them a sense of pride and an authentic voice to celebrate their beauty.

As it's plain to see, P&G's dedication to celebrating and promoting African-American beauty (and nurturing Black self-esteem) is stronger than ever. Beauty and self-confidence are, after all, innately connected. How better to kindle Black pride than to provide a national discourse by, for, and about Black women, their reflection in popular culture, and empowering them to serve as catalysts for positive change? The entrée came via the January 2009 *State of Black Beauty Survey*. A sample of 1,000+ African-American women, aged 18 to 54, responded to a self-administered online survey exploring their awareness and attitudes toward insights of African-American beauty and particularly the effect of the presidential election. The outcome was fascinating. Results from the 2007 survey had found that 77 percent of Black women were "concerned" about their portrayal in popular media. A majority of 71 percent expressed their portrayal in the media as "worse" than other racial groups, while 69 percent of respondents agreed that African-American teens are negatively impacted by such images.[3]

I cannot over-emphasize how important it is to intimately know your consumer, and what matters most to her. Research has shown that over two-thirds of African-American women felt "concerned" about media stereotypes, reporting that they were either portrayed in an inauthentic or unrealistic manner, or not reflected at all, particularly in the world of beauty and fashion. They also felt that their beauty needs were "underserved," with limited product formulations to meet their unique beauty needs. The limited distribution of those that do exist contributed to their struggle to find beauty products that work for them.

Considering these insights, the MBIB platform was a perfect vehicle to support African Americans in celebrating their beauty. Since self-confidence is inherently linked to self-image, the brand even came up with its own manifesto:

My Black is Beautiful

From the color of my skin, to the texture of my hair, to the length of my strands, to the breadth of my smile,

To the stride of my gait, to the span of my arms, to the depth of my bosom, to the curve of my hips, to the glow of my skin,
My Black is Beautiful

It cannot be denied. It will not be contained. And only I will define it.

For when I look in mirror, my very soul cries out,
My Black is Beautiful

And so today, I speak it out loud, unabashedly, I declare it anew,
My Black is Beautiful

Whether celebrated, imitated, exploited or denigrated. Whether natural from inside or skillfully applied,
My Black is Beautiful.

To my daughters, my sisters, my nieces, my cousins, my colleagues and my friends,

I speak for us all when I say again,
My Black is Beautiful.

Many Platforms

Over the past five years, the brand has engaged with consumers through a number of platforms including grass root community events such as the Essence Music Festival, sponsorships of key cultural events, social media engagement, community partnerships, and more. An entertainment extension of the campaign was on BET network's *My Black is Beautiful,* a show celebrating the diversity of African-American women in partnership with the P&G MBIB campaign, which encouraged them to promote their own beauty standard. With a celebrity cast that included actress and comedienne Kim Coles, television personality Alesha Renee, and actress Vanessa Williams, the show was warmly received.

The preeminent goal of MBIB is to encourage future generations to produce a new vision of self-actualization and to elevate the African-

American woman's portrayal in modern American culture. Sound like a tall order? Not when the integrated, multi-brand initiative is supported by Crest Pro-Health®, Pantene, Cover Girl Queen Collection®, Olay, and Always, along with an engaged Facebook community of more than 685,000 African-American women, Twitter, a dedicated website (myblackisbeautiful.com) and a number of brand activations throughout the year. Understanding the insight and need, P&G commitment has gone further to actually provide products designed for this growing demographic.

For a true insider's perspective on MBIB, I spoke at length with Verna Coleman-Hagler, brand manager at P&G. I wanted to take a close look at the origins of both MBIB and *Orgullosa* (Spanish for "proud"). Both programs were born out of the passion of P&G employees, specifically African-American women for MBIB and Latina women for *Orgullosa*. Coleman-Hagler explained, "We've historically had ethnic marketing run tangentially to the brand's marketing campaign and so there was a lot more passion (and even a little protection) around the programs because they were not necessarily integrated into the brand or product focus marketing. That really allowed each program to foster the spirit of what it means to activate behind a purpose. While *Orgullosa* has only been around for about a year, conceptually it was in the works for a couple of years. MBIB is in its fifth year, with market development time preceding its debut.

"For each person that works on it, myself included, there is a significant responsibility to protect the brand because of the focus on purpose. The purpose of each is centered around unleashing a positive transformation in the women that it serves. So, for MBIB it's focused on helping Black women express their true and best selves, and for *Orgullosa* it's for unleashing the transformative power of the community of Latinas. The purpose truly reflects the consumer." She said that the clear focus on the purpose helps maintain internal support as well as increasing consumer engagement.

Regarding *Orgullosa*, the 2010 Census showed that some 50.5 million (or 16 percent) of the U.S. population were of Hispanic origin, and P&G estimates that approximately 15 million Latinas share a dual (Latina and U.S.) heritage. Orgullosa.com celebrates this biculturalism and was launched during Hispanic Heritage month. Its mission is to celebrate the femininity of Latinas, while recognizing their dedicated spirit en route to personal and family success.

Getting back to purpose, when I asked about the ways of bringing it to life, of engaging communities, Coleman-Hagler said the programs have a laser focus on unmet needs. "For Black women, we knew that they felt very under-represented—in the ways they're shown in the media and in the ways they're perceived in everyday aspects of life. So, we massaged that insight to help us get to a purpose that will continue to flourish and be something that consumers want to engage with."

Coleman-Hagler continued, "And it's true for *Orgullosa* as well. We focus on the cultural aspect of Latinas and what we learned is:

- There's a stereotype of what a Latina is supposed to be: everything from her dress to her language to how she articulates in mixed company and what it means when she's speaking Spanish versus English. And there was this huge negative association that Latina women felt from other women.

- Also, this idea that being bi-cultural is really an asset to success, and that Latina women want to help each other see that biculturalism *is* an asset to success.

"Celebrating both these worlds—Spanish and English—that they inhabit really led us down the path toward transformative power of community because it is about women knowing that there's a lot of power in being bicultural. That," she emphasizes, "must be seen as something positive rather than something they have to fight against. We were able to marry the purpose against that unmet need in such a close fit that it helped each become very powerful and then the power of the purpose is what I think really engages consumers. For example, when we started *My Black is Beautiful,* it was simply called *Black is Beautiful.* Personalizing to *My* unleashed the campaign's power because women want to see themselves in the purpose. They want to know that it's for them and that's where building engagement starts. As well, social media helps them to further create a brand that's what they want it to be."

Perhaps you're wondering, as I was, about the importance of long-term presence for MBIB and Orgullosa. Coleman-Hagler talked about brand building. "Brands are experiences. I passionately believe that they are matters of the heart to consumers, hence the importance of maintaining a focus over a longer period of time so that consumers can get that full experience and develop fond associations. We've been able to maintain support and engagement from a consumer standpoint over a long period of time and we've had a lot of internal cheerleaders for the importance of the program—making sure that we don't have to see MBIB as promotional event, but rather, brand building."

There's a big difference. She continued, regarding the Latina initiative, "The same is true for Orgullosa. P&G understands the importance of building brands so we've been able to keep support by standing by the philosophy of the brand as experience. It takes time to build that brand with consumers and can't succeed as an in-and-out activity."

As for the right channels to drive engagement, Coleman-Hagler noted, "The most important tool is the current tool. Our tools are always current and shifts are always led by younger demographics. With the importance of social media, you now see a lot of everyday people becoming significant influencers because they're empowered (via social media) with 'megaphones' to give their opinions, their points of view, and to influence people in a big way beyond just their own circle of friends."

She said brands should ensure that their social media presence is personable, authentic, and feels like an experience that one consumer would have with another. "Brands are competing for a consumer's attention online, so when it comes to a brand that represents her, give it a voice she can relate to, a voice she'd expect from a friend or peer. This is a really strong 'unleashing' component of having a strong social media presence. And it's the most important component." Also, since social media is not a controlled environment, Coleman-Hagler stressed the importance of being flexible in letting that personality come through. "Even if it's a little off character for the brand," she confided, "consumers lead the way in social media."

I wanted her take on the best way for brands to measure the success of purpose-driven initiatives. "For us," she said, "it's really the participation, because if you have a strong purpose, sometimes that can be seen as a long-standing equity. Core metrics, the analytics, the Google searches and blogging, the social currency and conversation are important tools of course. All these things keep a pulse on the sentiment around your brand, along with the measurable aspects of sharing and developing content, in addition to all the things that a difference might measure if you're looking at top-line and bottom-line growth. The matters of the heart, however, are really about engagement and that's where purpose comes to life."

And what about profit? "Purpose," she reminded me, "is a pipeline to profit." If you're clear on purpose and you activate consistently, then you're bound to see a strong correlation to positive sales and ultimately, to profitability."

As for the future, Coleman-Hagler said brands need to do more to understand their customers. "For one thing, the landscape that faces multicultural consumers is changing so much on a daily basis. The impact of stereotypes or some of the negative influences or even the positive things that we may dismiss—the equalities and progress, for example—often we feel like we *know*, but we really should spend more time with the consumer. The second thing that everyone can do is to define who in the multicultural population you're focused on. It's hard to activate a purpose behind a big broad group of people—say, all African-American men or all Latinas—and still respect the diversity that exists within the multicultural population.

"That's a level of refinement, maybe sophistication, that I don't see happening a lot in today's marketplace. It's critical to broadly understand the consumer and then not be afraid to drill down to comprehend the nuances within the population. You can't just treat the whole population as one."

How Do You Inspire Your Audience?

By now I hope you're asking yourself some probing questions about your own consumer targets. How will you bring your brand purpose to life to meet their needs? Your company may have a promise in place, but what about a clearly defined, exciting purpose? What exactly will you do to inspire and activate your audience?

As Allen Adamson, author of *BrandDigital: Simple Ways Top Brands Succeed in the Digital World* and *BrandSimple: How the Best Brands Keep It Simple and Succeed,* (Palgrave Macmillan, 2009 and 2007) says, "Every brand makes a promise. But in a marketplace in which consumer confidence is low and budgetary vigilance is high, it's not just making a promise that separates one brand from another, but having a defining purpose."

With consumers flailing about in a Great Recession, desperately seeking the new normal, your *raison d'être* in terms of purpose has never been more important, for you or for them. Not to mention your shareholders. And, remember your employees, too. When things like price cuts are reinforced with purpose, your employees' position is more clearly defined, with the result that their role is seen as inherent to your brand. People thus vested are inspired to work harder for their company.

So, strive to contribute not only to shareholders but also to a broader purpose, because then and *only then* (as we've seen with *Make-a-Messterpiece* and *My Black is Beautiful*) do consumers form a true attachment with a brand.

TAKEAWAYS

1. Your purpose **must be unique**; must be authentic to your brand; the reason for your brand's existence

   • Why do you exist? What does your brand stand for? What do you want to stand for?

2. Your purpose **must be grounded in serving others**; your purpose comes to life through the service of others

   • How does purpose improve the lives of others?

3. Purpose must **start from the inside out**

   • Is there leadership commitment to your purpose? Does it inspire employees? Stakeholders? Customers?

4. Purpose comes to life through **co-creating with others**

   • Is your purpose meeting the needs of others?

   • Are you bringing it to life by co-creating with others?

Notes

1. www.artsusa.org
2. The Futures Company Multicultural Urban Study 2009; Urban Influencer Panel Series, Yankelovitch MONITOR Multicultural Study 2010.
3. myblackisbeautiful.com

Chapter 4

Serve People and the World

You have to find what sparks a light in you so that you in your own way can illuminate the world.

—Oprah Winfrey

PURPOSE IS A VEHICLE TO SERVE OTHERS and to best serve others you must get to know them. Intimate understanding of a typical day in the life of your customer is key to positioning your brand purpose. For those of you looking to connect at a more profound level with multicultural audiences, I think it starts within. Therefore having a workforce that mirrors your target audience in terms of multicultural diversity is the ideal. As we've seen, multicultural is the new mainstream. Without a diverse company roster, you risk the chance of coming up with solutions that are not relevant.

To take it a step further, if you're working with an agency, the same holds true for them. It's important to examine the diversity make-up in the agency's structure before signing on. The more diverse the personnel, the more likely it is that the agency will deliver work that will resonate with multicultural audiences. That said, don't be afraid to gather insights from within. As you can see from the previous chapter, a strong campaign such as the P&G *My Black is Beautiful* and *Orgullosa* was started from within. Passionate multicultural employees that are a part of the segment may have value added insight that could lead to your next big idea.

Don't work in a silo and rely on market research only. While we place an emphasis on market research and insights at our firm, we always do a "pulse check"—we invite leading influencers, community leaders, and potential targets to the discussion in order to understand what matters most. Be willing to put yourself in a day in the life of your customers. What did they do this morning? What beauty and personal products did they use before heading out the door? What brand of clothing did they put on? How did they wear it? How did it make them feel? Where do they receive their information on a daily basis—Twitter, blogs, online? And better yet, to push deeper: What matters to them? What do they desire out of life? What are their concerns? What issues are they facing? What are their challenges? The details, please.

All these questions and more need to be analyzed in terms of your customers, especially ones who are brand loyal. They're the ones who long to connect meaningfully with your brand and have it represent them. By so understanding, you can best align your brand purpose to meet an unmet need in the lives of your consumers, and watch your brand take off. But first, understand exactly where it fits in. Here are a few snap shots of a day in the life of multicultural consumers.

A Day in the Life Charts

NAME: **KENDRA**
AGE: **30**

I embrace my uniqueness inside and out, and invest time and money into looking good

I own a smart phone and like to connect with my social networks and social circles several times a day

I like brands that reflect my unique taste and individuality and generally remain brand loyal no matter what

I am focused on reaching the top of my career, looking good while getting there, and acquiring the brand badge to show it

I am very connected to my community and savvy advertisers can reach me at grassroots events.

I enjoy shopping and I tend to visit a variety stores and I am willing to pay more for quality. I also always keep up with the latest trends in fashion

I have a close circle of family and friends that look to me to plan gatherings and events as I enjoy hosting and introducing people to each other

I gravitate towards brands that show up in context in movies, TV shows, magazines and music

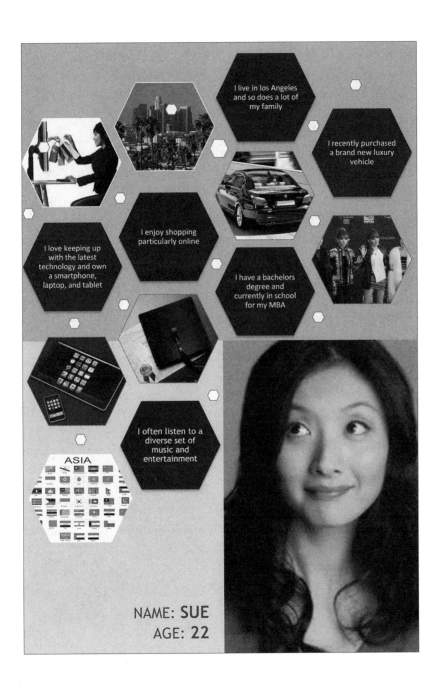

A Day in the Life Charts continued . . .

We often stay connected with my friends and family through social media via my phone or tablet

We look to media for entertainment as well as brand information

HABLA ESPAÑ

We like a stand out from the rest and express this through everything from clothes to music

NAME: **Perez Family**
AGES: **65, 62, 33, 32, 12, and 9**

We often prefer to speak English or Spanish language

As grandparents, we enjoy spending time with our family. We often stay connected with loved ones in our native country

We celebrate most holidays together and as often as we can we get together

NOTICIERO TELEMUNDO

It's a Brad Brad WORLD
New Series!
Mon, Jan 2 10/9c

We both graduated college and maintain careers that provide a combined income of $100K

We purchase and support Starbucks and Ben and Jerry and other brands that tend to support the LGBT community

We appreciate media that reflects our lifestyle choice and is not overt

We indulge in lavish purchases such as vacations and the latest technology

Larry and I dine out often, especially for social gathering with friends

We are very active in political and equal rights for the LGBT community. We often attend events in support of our community

NAMES: **LARRY AND STEVE**
AGES: **28 and 25**

A Day in the Life Charts continued . . .

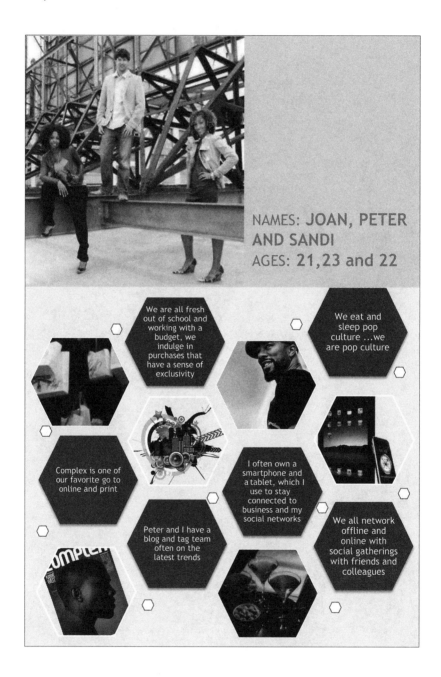

NAMES: **JOAN, PETER AND SANDI**
AGES: **21,23 and 22**

We are all fresh out of school and working with a budget, we indulge in purchases that have a sense of exclusivity

We eat and sleep pop culture ...we are pop culture

Complex is one of our favorite go to online and print

I often own a smartphone and a tablet, which I use to stay connected to business and my social networks

Peter and I have a blog and tag team often on the latest trends

We all network offline and online with social gatherings with friends and colleagues

Clearly, the future is multicultural.[1] In order to connect and bring your purpose to life to serve these growing markets you must first understand them and what matters most to them.

Know What Matters Most

Stay connected to what matters most to your consumer.
Look hard to uncover insight to emotionally connect.

Here's an example of a project that launched in July 2012: "Imagine a Future," brought to you by My Black is Beautiful with community partners Black Girls Rock! and United Negro College Fund (UNCF). I think this program is a perfect example of how an understanding of your consumer and what matters most to them can lead to a purpose-inspired platform. As you know from our previous chapter, My Black is Beautiful has entered its sixth year and has experienced success in building an engaged community of African-American women. Now it has to consider the next level.

Going back to the importance of uncovering insights and true understanding of the target, here is what we knew about our target Black woman, aged 18 to 54:

She is grounded in family values and self-confidence and her values come from an inter-generational connection that give her hope and strength to express her best self to the world. As Verna Coleman-Hagler noted earlier, we also know that she believes that media and companies should portray her more positively and showcase her in a positive light more often.

- 71% of Black women feel they are portrayed "worse" than women of other races in media.

- The consumer insight is that she defines her own beauty.

As we take a look deeper, we also know that she is very connected to community and seeks to leave her mark and ensure her community is cared for. She also cares about the next generation of young Black girls. This was something that rang true for me. A conversation came to my mind that I had with my family members a few months earlier (exact make-up of our target) along with an interesting dialogue with my younger cousin. She is a girl typical of her generation who faces challenges on the road to adulthood, particularly regarding her self image.

I was spending some time with family and getting reacquainted with my cousin Sherelle who I'd not seen in years. I also saw her daughter, Kennedy, who had grown into a beautiful young girl. I said, "Sherelle, Kennedy is absolutely gorgeous." My cousin replied, "Thanks Neshia, but try telling that to her; she doesn't think she is pretty at all." I inquired more and learned that my gorgeous young cousin did not feel beautiful because of the shade of her skin.

I was completely shocked and it was a real wake-up call regarding the type of self-esteem and confidence issues facing our young girls. This was a big emotional connection for me and I wanted to do something. I cared, but so did my cousin Sherelle (also the target). Sherelle was so adamant about doing something that she started an organization, Pretty Brown Girlz, in Atlanta, Georgia, a non-profit designed to provide curriculum to support young Black girls in feeling beautiful. Sherelle wanted to take action not only for Kennedy but also for the many young Black girls in Kennedy's network who struggled with self esteem, confidence, and feeling beautiful.

As I reflected on this conversation, I pondered the question, what matters to target? This was it—the typical African-American woman not only cared about having a place to express *her* authentic beauty, she also cared deeply about the next generation and the struggles of African-American girls. I've since followed up with a conversation with Kennedy.

Meet Kennedy: An Honest Discussion About Beauty

Here's what she had to say about being a teen and beautiful:

During the period when you struggled with self-esteem, tell us why you did not feel beautiful.

It started in the sixth grade, when I was adjusting to a new school environment. I felt that the lighter complexioned girls with long hair were prettier. So I thought that I was not pretty because of my

Some of my favorite celebrities are Beyonce, Carrie Underwood, Selena Gomez, Jennifer Hudson and Melanie Fiona

facebook

I usually spend 4 hours a day online connecting with friends on Facebook or playing games

NAME: **KENNEDY**
AGE: **14**
FRESHMAN AT DOUGLAS COUNTY HIGH SCHOOL
(DOUGHLASVILLE, GA)

I look to my Mother as my role model in my life

I am active in extracurricular activities at school such as cheerleading

I'm very into fashion and have my own unique style. When I grow up, I see myself becoming a fashion designer or model

I don't watch TV often, but when I do I mostly enjoy watching "Shake It Up" and "Wizards of Waverly Place" on the Disney Channel

DISNEP CHANNEL

complexion. I just felt ugly. Everybody said I was pretty but I didn't believe it. Boys preferred lighter-skinned girls—but you don't need a guy to tell you you're beautiful to be that way.

How did you rank your self-esteem back then; how do you rank it now?

This feeling ugly ended about eighth grade. I matured and realized I was beautiful both inside and out, but that inside was more important. I feel beautiful now because I have an uplifting personality and can help people feel better when they're down. On a scale of one to ten, in sixth grade I'd say my self-esteem was about three or four. Now, it's more like 7.5 or eight.

How do you define beautiful now?

Beauty is not just physical, but about personality, too.

Who are your role models? What entertainers or celebrities do you feel are beautiful?

My mother, because she is very pretty and I want to look like her. And my aunt, too. I also like Carrie Underwood, Beyoncé, Jennifer Hudson, and Melanie Fiona best.

Tell me a bit about some of the characters/shows that currently are shaping your definition of beauty?

I enjoy the Disney channel most of all, especially the show *Shake it Up,* where two friends of different races get along so well. One of them has dyslexia but still feels good about herself. Also, I like *The Wizards of Waverly Place* for Selena Gomez. But I'm not much of a TV person; Disney is all I watch.

What are your favorite websites?

I like Facebook to talk with friends. And I like games where you can design houses and clothes. I'd say I'm online about four hours daily.

What are your favorite stores?

Forever 21, 579, Body Central. I like clothes that other people don't have, especially if it's retro style.

What do you want to be when you grow up?

A fashion designer or model, something like that.

What advice would you give to a sixth-grade girl experiencing the problems you had at that age?

To be yourself; not try to be like anyone else. That's the best way to fit in. You don't have to be like everyone else to have friends.

. . .

After much discussion about Black women having a desire to support the next generation the MBIB "Imagine a Future" project was born. In 2012, at Essence Music Festival, My Black is Beautiful announced the next evolution of the MBIB movement:

> Through an exciting new partnership with Black Girls Rock! and United Negro College Fund, MBIB and partners joined forces on a new initiative called "Imagine a Future." The "Imagine a Future" initiative is a collaborative effort that will document the current state of Black beauty with an in-depth look at the influences—people, fashion, music, pop culture—of young Black girls. The initiative will provide tools and resources that positively impact the lives of one million Black girls over the next three years.

Ultimately, MBIB is engaging the community to imagine a future where every Black girl knows she is beautiful. This initiative not only celebrates the target's authentic beauty but also emotionally connects with her desire to pay it forward to make sure the next generation also feels beautiful.

When I think back on brainstorming with the brand, the community partners and agency teams were the perfect example of "purpose-inspired" people giving birth to "purpose-inspired" solutions. We actually ran around the room screaming. Yes! We were jumping up and down, filled with the excitement of how many young girls' lives could be improved and touched by a program like this. At one point in the brainstorm, I started going into one of my "inspirational" sermon-like speeches, saying this is evidence that creatives and marketers *can* make a difference, one campaign at a time.

Although the team laughed and said, "Oh my goodness, we have to listen to one of T's sermons," I wanted us to connect with the power of creative work when grounded in a "purpose" mindset. Once again, you want to have a creative team with desire and passion that are grounded in your brand's "purpose." Your team's inspiration must go well beyond something greater than your company's business results. And indeed the vision we had that day *was* much greater than that—we were re-imagining a more confident future for young Black girls everywhere. I'm honored to have been in the room with those great minds, and I'd like to think that all of us there were on a "purposeful" journey of using our creativity, branding, marketing and public relations skillset in a way to improve the world.

Causes That Matter Most

Another important question to ask: What causes and issues are most important to your consumer? After all, the glow of advertising dollars fades to grey in light of the reality of what consumers want, need, and believe in. They can see through a stodgy, generic mission statement in seconds and gravitate instead toward what's genuine, clearly articulated, and proven. As Rev. Run says, "People don't care what you know or what you're selling until they know who you are." Who are you? Multicultural consumers recognize values when they see them. What are yours?

It isn't a simple notion, far from it. As renowned speaker and strategic advisor Tom Asacker puts it, "It's what the consumer feels he is getting in exchange for his time, attention, and money that is decisive today. Value is determined using an internal feelings calculator, with simple functions like add and subtract, right and wrong, and more complex ones like weighing the outcome of one's decision on future achievement, affiliation, and contribution."

With that said, we will take a look at what societal issues are top of mind for these audiences, and what they value most. As we look at societal issues, for purpose-inspired projects, it's important to keep in mind that while cause-related platforms are *not* necessarily a must, they are great vehicles with which to marry your brand purpose to make a greater impact.

Across the spectrum of the broader multicultural audience, different causes and concerns arise more strongly than others. Here is a look at some leading causes that consumers care about within the U.S:

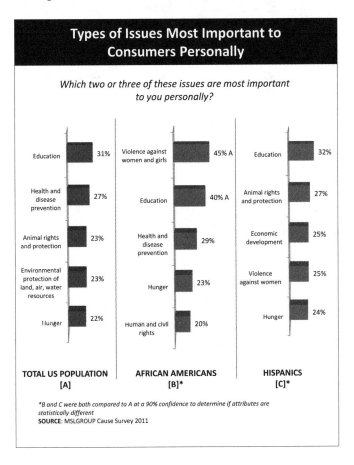

Types of Issues Most Important to Consumers Personally

Which two or three of these issues are most important to you personally?

TOTAL US POPULATION [A]

Issue	%
Education	31%
Health and disease prevention	27%
Animal rights and protection	23%
Environmental protection of land, air, water resources	23%
Hunger	22%

AFRICAN AMERICANS [B]*

Issue	%
Violence against women and girls	45% A
Education	40% A
Health and disease prevention	29%
Hunger	23%
Human and civil rights	20%

HISPANICS [C]*

Issue	%
Education	32%
Animal rights and protection	27%
Economic development	25%
Violence against women	25%
Hunger	24%

*B and C were both compared to A at a 90% confidence to determine if attributes are statistically different
SOURCE: MSLGROUP Cause Survey 2011

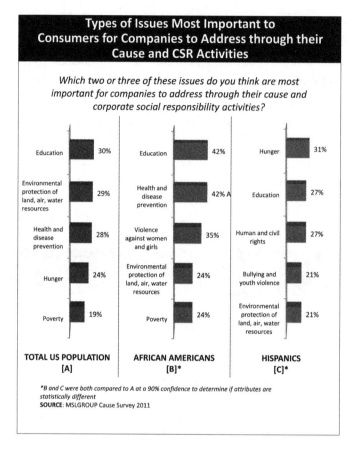

Types of Issues Most Important to Consumers for Companies to Address through their Cause and CSR Activities

Which two or three of these issues do you think are most important for companies to address through their cause and corporate social responsibility activities?

TOTAL US POPULATION [A]	AFRICAN AMERICANS [B]*	HISPANICS [C]*
Education — 30%	Education — 42%	Hunger — 31%
Environmental protection of land, air, water resources — 29%	Health and disease prevention — 42% A	Education — 27%
Health and disease prevention — 28%	Violence against women and girls — 35%	Human and civil rights — 27%
Hunger — 24%	Environmental protection of land, air, water resources — 24%	Bullying and youth violence — 21%
Poverty — 19%	Poverty — 24%	Environmental protection of land, air, water resources — 21%

*B and C were both compared to A at a 90% confidence to determine if attributes are statistically different
SOURCE: MSLGROUP Cause Survey 2011

Important Issues for Companies to Address

Like most of the U.S. population, African Americans and Hispanics also list education and environmental protection among the top five issues they consider most important for companies to implement in their cause/CSR efforts. Therefore, cause/CSR campaigns centered around education and/or the environment are an opportunity to reach both African-American and Hispanic communities at once.

Issues Important to African American Consumers

African Americans list education, health and disease prevention, and violence against women and girls as the top three issues they think companies should use for their cause/CSR efforts, and also as the top issues they personally find important. They are more likely than the general U.S. population to name health and disease prevention as an important issue for companies to address.

Implication: Consider implementing these three issues, specifically health and disease prevention, when engaging African Americans through cause/CSR efforts.

Issues Important to Hispanic Consumers

The issues Hispanics find important for companies to base their cause/CSR efforts on, and the issues they personally care about, mostly differ.

Implication: Companies should make efforts to help better the quality of life (e.g., education, hunger, human civil rights).

Implication: Issues they personally care about expand beyond that. Not only education and violence against women and girls, but animal rights and protection and economic development).

Education is the number one issue facing Blacks and Hispanics. Less than one-fourth of Latino men aged 18 to 24 were in enrolled in college or graduate school in 2009. The graduation rate of Black men is the lowest of any population—only 41 percent of Black males graduate high school nationwide.[2] Both *Black Enterprise* and the National Urban League have declared education within the African-American community to be in a state of emergency. In the inner cities, more than half of all Black men do not finish high school.[3] This is not an issue peculiar to multicultural audiences; it is an American issue given its effect on crime rates and other issues. Therefore, if this is an area you choose to support, it could resonate beyond the multicultural to your general market platforms as well.

It's one thing to care about these issues, another to incorporate them into a marketing campaign, especially when factoring in elements such as DSM (digital social media). Ask yourself: Is our content socially, culturally and distinctly relevant? For multicultural audiences, this is a particularly important consideration. These questions need to be addressed in a meta-level campaign that includes social networking media (predominantly Facebook and Twitter). As marketing executive Troy Brown, founder and CEO of one50one LLC, puts it, "our (multicultural) consumption patterns and habits are greatest in terms of growth of consumption of all media across DSM."

Indeed, African-American, Hispanic, and Asian-American consumers are known to download more games, mobile ringtones, and images than Whites. They consume a wider range of mobile media and share shopping and entertainment advice, too. And, most importantly, 48 percent of consumers use social media such as Facebook and Twitter to support causes. The top uses of social media, in order of importance, to support causes are:

1. Learn and stay informed

2. Connect with others concerned about the same issue

3. Show friends/network what causes care about

4. Share opinions about the causes companies should support

5. Share existing content[4]

In a marketplace exploding with options, some brands have succeeded in identifying leading causes among multicultural consumers and creating vehicles to bring their brand purposes to life by meeting a need within the immediate life of their customers and their communities. A **brand's power** is, after all, derived from the **goodwill** and **name recognition** that it has **earned** over time, translating into higher **sales volume** and higher **profit margins** against competitors.

Let's take a look at the Hennessy Artistry campaign of 2010.

For over five years, Hennessy delivered a concert-type experience within key multicultural markets targeted to urban consumers aged 21 to 29. Hennessy understood the passion points of this consumer, creating a unique experience that leveraged the arts, culture, and music—the perfect platform to connect meaningfully with them. Going into the fifth year of the campaign, the brand's executive leadership knew it was the perfect time to elevate the platform with meaning and cause.

Taking the process seriously, the brand team did not just jump aboard the latest sexy-cause bandwagon. Their intention, first and foremost, was loyalty to the equity and the distinguished history of the brand. Hennessy already had a number of programs in support of its goal of fostering and preserving ethnic culture. The executives believed in generously giving back to the community and promoting the importance of responsible consumption, with a passion for the community dating back to 1896. That's when William Jay Schieffelin, founder of Schieffelin & Co. (now Moët Hennessy USA) joined the Tuskegee Institute (now Tuskegee University) Board of Directors and encouraged many Northern industrialists to support the school. Schieffelin was also aggressive in fighting the KKK—a cause few back then were willing to take on. From 1896 until today, the company has continued to support multicultural communities through a wide range of initiatives and community donations. Thus, it was only natural for them now to add meaning and cause to their leading consumer engagement platform—Hennessy Artistry.

Hennessy Artistry is a global music campaign to promote the art of mixing various genres and blending the talents of the world's top artists. Every trademark Hennessy Artistry event is an evening of unification, blending sound, visual innovation, and drinking experiences from around the world. Each event features some of the hottest and most cutting-edge names in music today. We determined we could leverage the

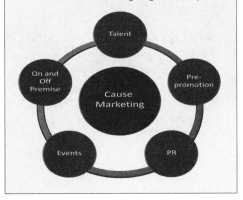

Cause Marketing Threads Through all Components of Hennessy Artistry

Cause Marketing
- Threads through all program components
- Talent promotes via press and social media
- Print, radio, on-line and mobile champion our cause
- Good will is shared via all media releases
- Donation/give back at events
- POS directs to mobile giving and sweeps

Talent

On and Off Premise

Pre-promotion

Cause Marketing

Events

PR

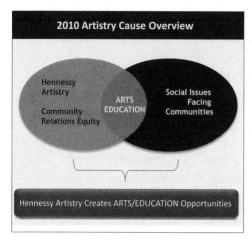

brand's long-standing history of supporting education into this existing platform by supporting arts education.

We created a new component of the tour, Artistry Gives. The brand partnered with the leading arts education resource, Americans for the Arts (AFTA), to locate deserving artists within each market, and created an ownable Hennessy Grant Program titled Artistry Gives, which gives Hennessy Artistry Community Grants (HACG). Blending music, arts, and culture with the art of giving, the

Hennessy is the master of blending the best the world has to offer.

In the spirit of innovation, blending and creativity, Hennessy Artistry 2010 combined music, culture, art and cause to bring consumers unforgettable experiences.

HACG provides emerging artists of color with grants and scholarship opportunities to further their arts education. It does this by awarding grants to non-profit arts organization within each of the Hennessy Artistry markets: Chicago, Detroit, Miami, New York, and Los Angeles. Also, Hennessy Artistry and AFTA, along with a local non-profit grant recipient commissions an emerging artist to document the Artistry experience and enjoy the opportunity to showcase his or her work at Hennessy Artistry events nationwide.

The blend of arts, culture, and giving was woven throughout each element. The cause element, with the insight that the average urban consumer is online up to five hours each day, looked for ways to provide those consumers with online engagement opportunities. For every "like" on the Facebook Hennessy Artistry page, one dollar was donated to Americans for the Arts—up to $25,000. This allowed consumers to be active, to share in the narrative, and be provided with tools to mobilize their networks and a badge to share with them. They could easily post within their social media platforms with a call to action to join the cause. It's important to provide your consumers with the tools to advocate within their personal networks. Let them own the cause, and further empower them to personalize it through their own advocacy. "Give us the tools," as Winston Churchill said to FDR, "and we will finish the job."

Jenay Alejandro, Associate Manager of Multicultural Relations at Moët Hennessy USA, shared some key learnings Hennessy has gathered when connecting with multicultural communities through purpose.

Community/Cause are Great Vehicles to Bring Your Brand Purpose to Life

As Alejandro puts it, "Find a community partner who understands the brand and who can translate that into community events and initiatives." That way, according to Alejandro, the company's reputation in a community strengthens the brand in the long-term. Frankly, if you're not involved with cause and community, you can expect to see a downturn in your business.

Do the research. Don't make the mistake of just donating money without tracking where exactly it goes. "As a brand, you always have to be prepared to say, for example, we gave $30,000 to the New York Urban League and it went to support six students and five technology assistance programs and things of that nature." Don't just examine which trends are "hot" for the moment as opposed to what is truly resonating with a given community, e.g., education over entrepreneurship. A strong local reputation in a community, after all, strengthens the brand in the long term. Professional organizations like African-American MBAs or Hispanic MBAs are important for the luxury aspect of a brand like Moët Hennessy.

Understanding What Matters Most to Your Consumer

In addition to doing quantifiable surveys and focus group research, Hennessy does trade nights and actually just sits and talks to people about what they're drinking and why, said Alejandro. She continued, "And we listen to our salespeople, those valiant souls on the front lines, and take *their* lead as to what's happening at the street level. Based on research, for example, we know that the three most important passion touch points for the African-American and Latino communities that closely align with our brand community relations equity are arts, education, and civil rights (i.e., continued access to opportunity). There is a concentrated focus on issues that fit Hennessy as a corporation: art, education, luxury. And that's a major part of how we align with the causes that most appeal to our consumers."

The Value of Cause/Purpose with Multicultural Consumers

Alejandro said, "Today, you're running the risk of lost credibility if you don't have some sort of a cause or purpose component to your marketing. Tapping into an applicable cause gives you the competitive edge. That's what creates a meaningful relationship. You're also tapping into people's emotions, where they feel good about the purchase and where you're not, in terms of brand, interchangeable. When consumers are so inundated with technology and messages, and you're able to pick that applicable cause and be really strategic about sharing it with your consumer, then you have a competitive edge in a really organic way."

Education is the most important cause in the multicultural community. Not only is it in a state of emergency, but it's also cross-cultural and taps into universal beliefs about a basic right and the key to economic mobility. "I do see causes that resonate differently between multicultural and general market," she continued. "If you look at the general market, many of the purpose initiatives are international in reach. However, at Hennessy we keep our cause efforts beneficial to U.S. consumers and *that* resonates powerfully. When you're giving out Thurgood Marshall scholarships in their own neighborhoods, it resonates deeply with people who might not have access to education, especially versus a far-off African charity."

I felt that her last comment really connected back to the key insight about Hennessy understanding its core consumer. Alejandro agreed, saying, "International causes can be really star-studded, ringing all the bells and whistles that you want for things like amfAR and Keep a Child Alive. But we try to ensure that the vast majority of activation keeps the money at home, in the communities that matter most to us."

Keeping Long-standing Partnerships "Hot"

I wondered how Hennessey creates new programs with old partners. Alejandro said, "We have meetings with our legacy partners and examine targets that we're innovating towards. For example, we've worked with the Urban League for one hundred years and, while we support their standard programming, we've also supported their New York Young Urban League Professionals division because working with that group gave us more credibility and was closer to what the marketing campaign was going after. So, some of it is just seeing how the organization is evolving and staying on top of that.

"When you look at an NAACP, at an Urban League or Hispanic Federation, they are all service agencies that help to support smaller cause marketing non-profits. For example, the Hispanic Federation has

92 service agencies that they work with, and I can look at those service agencies and decide where this year's efforts will be directed—perhaps, this year financial literacy, and next year green initiatives for Latinos. When you have an organization like that, they are evolving with you and adding new agencies or opportunities for engagement. The Northern Manhattan Arts Alliance was actually an incubation project from the Hispanic Federation. I felt they were getting involved with the arts in Washington Heights and that was a home run for us.

"I encourage anyone in cause marketing," she added, "to look at established organizations. Up-and-coming groups can be very interesting and sexy, but you must be cognizant of the tried and true. They've got the system down, they've dealt with corporate, and they know what you need."

Regarding the sensitive area of what makes a corporate community partnership authentic and credible, Alejandro pointed out that "It's got to be something that speaks to your brand on the corporate side." On the other side of the coin, "in terms of the community, it has to be just as exciting for them. Not just another check, presentation, or hoop to jump through, but a real desire to create a long-term partnership."

When it comes to community partners, Alejandro has some simple criteria. "We like to stick to the U.S., to people who are serving the target demographic and are sufficiently established, with a track record, with good standing finances, taxes filed, and things of that nature. They must jive with our strategy, have influence, and do good work."

Driving ROI at Hennessy with Purpose

What are the best ways for brands to measure success and ROI of purpose-driven marketing against these community partnerships? "A solid way to quantify it is always through the communications piece, the PR and media impressions. Depending on what the activation is, you can track sales. Four years ago," she related, "we tracked sales along the West Indian parade route in Brooklyn, where we were major sponsors. Sales went up 46 percent. Depending on what you do, you can do some surveying and some tracking and some conversion rate, but it's really an attitude." And, she said, don't discount results that take a year or more to appear. That's when community leaders will support you as a corporation, when you've proven your consistency. And even though there's not a number value, it is invaluable for what it can do from a PR perspective, especially if you ever find yourself painted into a corner.

The Future of Community/Purpose at Hennessy

As for future engagement with the multicultural community, Alejandro suggests, "Doing research, having a clear strategy and tight, clear-cut approach as to how you're going to engage the community is crucial, as opposed to just throwing things against the wall and seeing what sticks. Instead, brands need to continue to do more to uplift consumers and call on them as equal partners, rather than talking down to them, or telling them a story as outsiders."

Secret Deodorant Bases Social Media Campaign on New Users

Another great campaign that originated as the result of a brand's deep insight into the lives of their consumers was Secret Deodorant's *Mean Stinks*. Secret's purpose is tied directly to a woman's right to live fearlessly. Insights led to the brand's realization that the onset of puberty can coincide with the onset of bullying and it is at the same time that a young woman is starting to use deodorant products. Over the past few years, bullying has become a number-one issue in the United States, directly (or indirectly) leading to an estimated 4,400 deaths yearly in our country alone.

Secret responded with the *Mean Stinks* campaign and watched its Facebook fans *and* sales took off. In August 2011, *Advertising Age* reported:

> Since launching the "Mean Stinks" program, which has also included a publicity tie-in with *Glee*'s Amber Riley and an iAd campaign launched last month, Secret's already strong sales growth kicked up a notch. The brand had momentum anyway, with a

current streak of 17 consecutive quarters of share growth, according to P&G. Sales are up 8% to around $250 million in channels tracked by SymphonyIRI for the 52 weeks ended July 10, but they're up an even faster 9% for the 26 weeks ended June 26, a period affected by the "Mean Stinks" campaign that launched in January on Facebook. Secret, already the leading U.S. deodorant, saw its share rise 0.6 points for the past 52 weeks and 0.7 points for the first half of 2011.

Setting up an interactive community called *Mean Stinks* on Facebook, Secret created a safe place that gave girls access to experts, tips, tools, and resources for coping with bullies, or even to identify any bullying tendencies in themselves. The page offers repentant bullies an opportunity to apologize via video as well, inspiring all page visitors to courageously face the challenges associated with aggressive behavior. They also partnered with PACER's National Bullying Prevention Center by donating a portion of the proceeds from select Secret Clinical Strength purchases—i.e., those made with an online coupon available through the Facebook page—to PACER's prevention efforts.

A key aspect of the campaign was allowing consumers to own it, and also partnering with role models like Amber Riley (star of *Glee*) and nationally renowned relationship expert, Rachel Simmons. Amber and Rachel align with the *Mean Stinks* program vision of empowering young women to stand against what stinks (bullying) and undertake a movement of "nice." This a superb example of a strong call to action allowing powerful consumer engagement.

Five Simple Rules

To sum this chapter up, I think we can learn a lot from a market leader. Your first move, as a purpose-driven marketer, is to hold fast to these five simple rules as outlined by Procter & Gamble's Global Marketing Officer Marc Pritchard at the October 2010 ANA Conference: *Defining Purpose*:

1. It starts with each brand defining its *purpose.*

   "We expect every one of our brands to be guided by a purpose that defines how it uniquely touches and improves lives. We think of it as the soul of the brand."

2. *Reinforcing* the Brand's Core **Benefit**

   ". . . and that purpose springs from and reinforces the essence of the brand's core benefit. So at the end of the day, while people will buy into a purpose, they buy a benefit . . ."

3. *Serving* People with Brands

   "But, the great thing about a purpose is that it can open up new possibilities to deliver that benefit to consumers. It means shifting our mindset from marketing to serving. That means changing from marketing *to* people—so we get them to do what we want them to do which is buy our products—to *serving* people with our brands to make their lives better. And that can take many forms: of course, it's better products; but it's also non-product services; it's entertainment that brings people together; and it's acts of kindness and generosity that have them part of the larger community . . ."

4. *Insights* on People

   "It also means thinking of who we serve as people. Now this may seem obvious, but when we have a mindset of marketing to consumers, it leads to a focus of getting them to try to do what we want them to do: consume our products. But, when we focus on serving people, we're forced to gain a deeper understanding about their whole lives and give them what they want to make their entire life better. And when we focus on serving people, we uncover human insights. Not product insights. Deep human insights that define the essence of human behavior. They represent universal human truths, motivations and tensions that must be solved by the benefits of our brands. And from these insights we create big ideas . . ."

5. *The Big Idea*

"Big ideas are the currency of our industry. Big ideas have to lift the entire brand and make it relevant in people's lives. Lift the entire brand—and not just the product initiatives that we've proliferated over the course of the last 10 years. Big ideas that ARE so engaging and surprising that they invite people to participate in our brand communities and that can take many forms from word-of-mouth advocacy and PR, to passing along YouTube videos, to engaging fans on Facebook, to getting on the website, to making a donation to charity, and, of course, participation means purchase. The key is that people become personally associated with the brand and then become loyal members of the community, and even ambassadors."

. . .

Maybe now is a good time to ask yourself: what causes among multicultural consumers have caught your attention lately? How could your company step in? Bear in mind some more important statistics: 93 percent of consumers want to know what companies are doing to make the world a better place and 91 percent want companies to hear their views. An unfortunately high 71 percent report feeling confused by the message companies use to discuss their efforts and impacts.[5]

Therefore, brands need to be clear and concise with their messaging and ensure that the cause selected makes sense in the minds of consumers. It's key to understand which causes activate people to action if your ultimate goal is engagement.

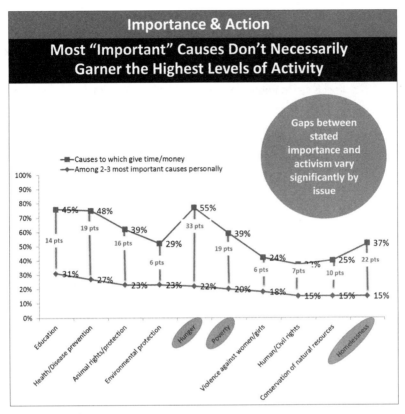

Importance & Action

Most "Important" Causes Don't Necessarily Garner the Highest Levels of Activity

Gaps between stated importance and activism vary significantly by issue

- Causes to which give time/money
- Among 2-3 most important causes personally

Education 45%, 31%, 14 pts
Health/Disease prevention 48%, 27%, 19 pts
Animal rights/protection 39%, 23%, 16 pts
Environmental protection 29%, 23%, 6 pts
Hunger 55%, 22%, 33 pts
Poverty 39%, 20%, 19 pts
Violence against women/girls 24%, 18%, 6 pts
Human/Civil rights 25%, 15%, 7pts
Conservation of natural resources 25%, 15%, 10 pts
Homelessness 37%, 15%, 22 pts

Not all causes garner activity. Take a close look at each cause and have a simple call to action.

As you come up with your campaign, be very strategic in terms of its providing balance between local and global, between giving and receiving, between passive and actually allowing consumers to be activated.

The point here is that bringing a purpose to life can have many different aspects. Your consumer engagement may take different forms—volunteering time, social media posting, donations, and product purchases.

In the Current Environment, Successful CSR Campaigns Require a Fine Balance

Importance
"Pass"ivism
PSR
Global
Giving

Action
Activism
CSR
Local
Receiving

TAKEAWAYS

1. Purpose is a vehicle to serve others and **to best serve others you must get to know them.** Intimate understanding of a typical day in the life of your customer is key to positioning your brand purpose. For those of you looking to connect at a more profound level with multicultural audiences, I think it starts within, and therefore having a workforce that mirrors your target audience in terms of multicultural diversity is the ideal.

2. **Don't work in a silo and rely on market research only.** While we place an emphasis on market research and insights at our firm, we always do a "pulse check"—we invite leading influencers, community leaders, and potential targets to the discussion in order to understand what matters most. Be willing to put yourself in a day in the life of your customers.

3. You need to have **a creative team with desire and passion** that are grounded in your brand's "purpose." Your team's inspiration must go well beyond something greater than your company's business results.

4. Another important question to ask: What causes and issues are most important to your customer? After all, the flow of advertising dollars fades to grey in light of the reality of what consumers want, need, and believe in. They can see through a stodgy, generic mission statement in seconds and gravitate instead toward what's **genuine, clearly articulated, and proven**.

Notes

1. McClellan Tesar Reynes, LLC Research for Diversity and Integrated Marketing Communications. Reprinted from DMA in *Marketing Magazine,* January 2006.
2. Schott Foundation for Public Education.
3. *The New York Times,* March 20, 2006.
4. 2011 MSLGROUP.
5. 2011 Cone/Echo Global CR Study.

Chapter 5

Celebrities Gone Good

As we look ahead into the next century, leaders will be those who empower others.

—Bill Gates

HISTORICALLY, celebrity endorsement is far from a new invention—even in the 19th century, Queen Victoria was lending her name to increase sales for Cadbury's cocoa—but not until 1984 was celebrity power harnessed on a mass scale to spotlight a particular cause. That's when Band Aid, Bob Geldof's legendary conglomerate of rock superstars, took to the airwaves with the hit "Do They Know It's Christmas?" in support of famine relief in Ethiopia. Since then, charities and brands have become ever more sophisticated in their methods for reaching a wide audience by mining society's passion for celebrity.

In fact, if you had to free associate the words "celebrity" and "cause," what are some of the first names that spring to mind? Gloria Gaynor, Cynthia Nixon, and Ebony Steele for the Susan G. Komen Foundation; Cindy Crawford, Hayden Panettiere, and Carl Lewis for Ronald McDonald House. Any more? How about Alicia Keys for Keep a Child Alive; Halle Berry, Dwayne Johnson, and Miley Cyrus for the Make-A-Wish Foundation; Natalie Morales, and Jewel for The March of Dimes; Rodney, and Holly Robinson Peete for the Hollyrod Foundation benefiting autism and Parkinson's disease. Then there are the stand-alone names, those that have become synonymous with celebrity and charitable causes: Angelina Jolie, Bono, Oprah Winfrey, George Clooney, Ellen DeGeneres, Bill Gates, and Elton John. Any way you slice it, social responsibility is a hot trend that just gets hotter. And having a substantial purpose is no longer just admirable; it's downright sexy.

Stars, already known to shape destinies, cast an enormous influence. This isn't anything to do with astrology. I'm referring to the powerful effect of celebrities on brand destinies. One approving nod from the "right" famous face can translate into millions in brand sales.

But it is equally important to look beyond the big names and splashy sales scenarios. Do celebrity endorsements always work? What groundwork needs to be in place before such a relationship yields profits? As with any leap into emotional branding, you need to take a good look first at who your celebrity really is and what he or she stands for.

A possible downside? Just think of Tiger Woods. Or Michael Vick. Or Kobe Bryant. When celebrities attract scandal to their names, their endorsements suffer. More subtly, a celebrity must have a direct connection to the brand he or she is endorsing, like Michael Jordan for Air Jordan sneakers. Jordan was a legendary athlete and his footwear was critical to his performance. Easy. But what about the Donald Trump signature collection for Macy's menswear? Did that go anywhere? Not really. Trump's connection is to real estate, not suits. More people look at his hair anyway. And whatever celebrities you may be looking at—for a brand partnership or cause spokesperson—they have to be examined closely as a good fit in all areas, especially personal image and brand connection.

Social media is also a vital extension of any celebrity's brand and has to be respected as such. When they mention a brand name on their network, it has to feel authentic and natural. Celebrities may provide an exciting kick-off for a word-of-mouth campaign because of their vast numbers of fans. However, is this really an authentic way to engage an audience? I'm frankly not positive that paying a celebrity $10,000 per tweet, or a Facebook update, will influence an audience or be part of a scalable social media strategy, especially if the celebrity has not expressed his passion in his own words.

But when the right celebrities, causes and brands come together, magic happens.

I learned this early on in my urban culture experiences. As I've already mentioned, it's no surprise to anyone that Russell Simmons was in the vanguard of asking the big question: What is hip-hop's purpose in serving the world *and* in serving as a catalyst for change. In 2001, along with Dr. Benjamin Chavis, Russell founded the Hip-Hop Summit Action Network (HSAN), a non-profit, non-partisan national coalition of hip-hop artists, entertainment industry leaders, civil rights proponents, and youth leaders dedicated to exploiting the cultural relevance of hip-hop music as a catalyst for education advocacy and other societal concerns fundamental to the empowerment of youth.

As mentioned earlier, one of my first projects was working closely with the HSAN, the National Urban League, and the Verizon Foundation to launch Hip-Hop Reader. Following that successful undertaking, Simmons asked me to serve as project manager to lead a  venture near and dear to his heart: HSAN's Get Out the Vote campaign. A powerful teaching experience for me in terms of celebrity power, the project would later serve as a guide for working with the famous to deliver purpose-inspired programs. The major insight gleaned from Get Out the Vote was that working with passionate "celebrities gone good" could deliver exciting programming that yielded success for both brands and communities.

HSAN's Get Out the Vote project involved nationwide travel, hosting concert-like events in packed arenas filled with young adults, live music, A-list celebrities such as Jay-Z, Beyoncé, Eminem, Nelly, P. Diddy, Ludacris, Kanye West, Will Smith, Nick Cannon, and LL Cool J, all to discuss the importance of voting. Yes, you read that correctly. Standing room only venues filled with young people seeking empowering knowledge from their own trusted icons. The year was 2004, and Simmons (along with HSAN) sponsored a 12-city tour to rally communities to exercise their voices and power by casting their ballots to vote. Completely non-partisan and unallied with any political party, the HSAN

mission was as single minded as it gets: to register young adults nationwide to vote.

However, certain brands were keen to take part served as lead sponsors. Playstation and Anheuser-Busch were among HSAN's title brand
sponsors to create the tour. Each city event was hosted by an iconic
celebrity native to that particular town, along with community leaders. As we traveled the country, Beyoncé hosted Houston, Kanye West
joined us in Chicago, Nelly hosted St. Louis, and Snoop Dogg hosted
Los Angeles. The tour was featured in every major news outlet from
CNN to the *New York Times, USA Today* and more. As Simmons told
CNN,

> The collective consciousness of hip-hop is rising. There's no ques-
> tion about that. Everyone from Jay-Z to Puffy to Beyoncé to
> Eminem. They all show up at Hip-Hop Summits, and they all
> contribute not only their celebrity and time but their actual money
> to efforts to uplift their community. There is a trend of rappers'
> giving back. Will Smith hosted a summit with LL Cool J and
> others in Philly and registered 80,000 voters. Beyoncé hosted her
> summit in Houston. Master P., Puffy, Reverend Run, and Ice
> Cube came to that summit and registered 25,000 to 30,000 vot-
> ers. Snoop Dogg, Damon Dash, and others hosted the L.A. event
> and brought in 60,000 voters. And the mayors of all these cities
> were involved.

At each summit, youth would rally, the DJ would spin as the audience entered the venue, and our brand sponsor would engage with the
youth via polls, product giveaways, and e-blasts. The artists came on
stage; some would start out rhyming, some dancing, some by hyping
the crowd. But ultimately they all shared their personal stories of the
importance of making their voices known in the most powerful way
of all, by voting. After hearing these personal stories, the audience was
invited to ask questions and voice their own opinions. Occasionally
there were moments of great honesty when artists confessed to not
having voted before. Then, they would register on-site, along with the
attendees. As you can imagine, it was a powerful moment when an artist

registered for the first time, publicly. They were setting a vivid example for their fans, and those of us who were there witnessed real life growth and evolution of the culture.

Left: P. Diddy and Kweisi Mfume

Two months prior to election day 2004, HSAN created the Freedom Ride bus tour, traveling through the Northeast and Midwest, visiting 26 cities in 10 states. As Simmons said, the tours were designed to remind people of the Freedom Rides of the 1960s, when young African-American people fought to defend their voting rights. P. Diddy exclaimed, "Young voters in this country are throwing away their power to have a say about education, health care, and any issue that affects them. These things affect you, so vote or die!" Vote or Die became the rallying cry. The campaign enjoyed huge success, registering over 1.8 million youth in an achievement that dramatically foreshadowed the presidential election just four years later. The tour generated over 200 million media impressions and created a true Rosa Parks moment for the 21st century.

During the campaign, there were more than a few moments when I knew that I was witnessing a cultural movement that had the potential to effect profound change; change such as Martin Luther King Jr. had envisioned. Some of the participants referred to the summits as the Civil Rights movement of our time. One night, in the middle of a Miami housing project, we appropriated the common areas, providing seating for all the residents. With jumbo screens erected, we played inspiring messages from community leaders and celebrity ambassadors, encouraging the audience to make their voices heard. Voter registration occurred on the spot and at that moment it was clear to me that the power of urban culture, though still in its infancy, was able to effect great change.

These celebrities all donated their time. This wasn't about money for them, but a higher purpose that transcended financial gain. It was about exercising their power to effect change regarding leading issues facing their fans, their communities, and their own blocks. This project proved to me that celebrities and influencers who are "personally" engaged and share a "passion" for your brand purpose can be your greatest asset to do great works in the world. This presentation was so successful that HSAN continued to model the format to advocate and deliver empowering platforms.

Get Your Money Right

Simmons made debt consolidation a topic as hot as voting when he orchestrated the two-year *Get Your Money Right* financial empowerment tour. HSAN, along with title sponsor Chrysler Financial and presenting sponsor Anheuser-Busch, Inc., produced a seven-city event that touched key multicultural markets, resulting in thousands of attendees. In response to bad credit, spiraling debt, and financial mismanagement in our communities, HSAN continued its tour for a second year. That tour featured a panel discussion moderated by Dr. Benjamin Chavis, President/CEO of HSAN and included Simmons, hip-hop stars Rev. Run, Chingo Bling, Slim Thug, Belly, and Short Dawg, along with R&B/pop stars Monica, LaToya Luckett, Solange Knowles, and Lady Lux. The *Get Your Money Right* agenda highlighted an interactive panel discussion on all aspects of personal financial management, with a *Get Your Money Right* workbook in both English and Spanish. Special programs were offered for high school students.

The *Get Your Money Right* tour also teamed up with Walmart for a presentation pinpointing a variety of financial issues, acknowledging that financial literacy is critical, especially when multicultural communities are disproportionately affected by the economic downturn. As Simmons said, "The recession continues to hit the minority communities the hardest and without financial literacy, those communities will not be able to move forward to improve their standards of living." For Walmart, partnering with HSAN in this

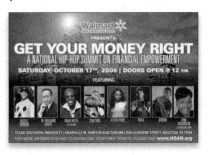

action was an opportunity to extend its own core mission to help people save money so that they can live better. Celebrities Russell Simmons, BET's Alesha Renée, Free, and Slim Thug ensured high entertainment value as well, with many of the artists sharing their own personal financial stories.

Later, these tours were followed by yet another: the *Get Your House Right* home-ownership tour, an initiative with sponsor Genworth Financial to provide solutions to the multi-billion dollar mortgage and foreclosure crisis facing young Americans. Another A-list group of celebrities participated, led by mortgage guru Lynn Richardson, former vice president of national strategic partnerships for JPMorgan Chase and author of *Living Check to Monday: The Real Deal About Money, Credit and Financial Security* (Lynn Richardson Enterprises, Inc., 2005). The tour included consumer workshops, home buyer pavilions, and an advisory panel of industry experts offering home ownership tools, tips and counseling, and generally demystifying the home buying process and real estate investment.

Simmons has pushed to have urban culture explore its role as a catalyst for change and inspired others to run with the baton. This trend has continued to grow, given that so many artists/celebrities have now adopted social responsibility and become passionate about leaving their mark. There's ample opportunity to partner with celebrities in doing good works.

TAKEAWAYS

1. Charities and brands have become ever more sophisticated in their methods for reaching a wide audience by mining society's passion for celebrity. Any way you slide it, **social responsibility is a hot trend** that just gets hotter. And having a substantial purpose is no longer admirable, it's downright sexy.

2. It is equally important to look beyond the big names and splashly sales scenarios. Do celebrity endorsements always work? No. What groundwork needs to be in place before such a relationship yields profits? As with any leap into emotional branding, you need to **take a good look first** at who your celebrity really is and what he or she stands for.

3. Social media is also a vital extension of any celebrity's brand and has to be respected as such. When they mention a brand name on their network, **it has to feel authentic and natural**.

Chapter 6

Get to Know Celebrities with Purpose

In helping others, we shall help ourselves, for whatever good we give out completes the circle and comes back to us.

—Flora Edwards

Phillip Bloch talks up Cause Celeb

LONG CONSIDERED one of Hollywood's premier fashion stylists, Phillip Bloch has played the role of style ambassador at Fashion Weeks in the U.S. and internationally. With clients such as Halle Berry (who he dressed for the Emmys, SAG Awards, and Oscars), Drew Barrymore, Sandra Bullock, Mariah Carey, Jim Carrey, Salma Hayak, Nicole Kidman, Michael Jackson, Jennifer Lopez, and more, he is arguably one of Hollywood's most important fashion figures. Ever ahead of the curve, and a master of influential brand building, Bloch hosts the popular *Cause Celeb* broadcast segments for *ABC News*.

His insider access to all things show business, as well as his devotion to philanthropy, led him to create *Cause Celeb*. Focusing on various celebrities and their causes, *Cause Celeb with Phillip Bloch* features celebrity interviews with the likes of Fran Drescher (Cancer Schmancer); Cee Lo Green (Duracell's commitment to the Power Those Who Protect

Us program supporting the National Volunteer Fire Council); Jordin Sparks (VH1's Save the Music Foundation); Andie MacDowell (L'Oréal's The Color of Hope, supporting the Ovarian Cancer Research Fund); Ben Stiller (Stiller Foundation and Worldwide Orphans Foundation); and Christie Brinkley (Danskin's Move for Change initiative benefiting breast cancer).

When I had the chance to sit down and talk with the über-expressive Bloch about his work, both tears and laughter punctuated our conversation. First, I asked about the road that led to Cause Celeb and he sketched in the beginnings of his purpose-led journey. "In my teens and early twenties," he said frankly, "I was modeling and it was all about my looks. In my late twenties and thirties, I was a celebrity stylist and it was all about other people's looks but still superficial—their dresses, their premiers, etc. I did it more for the legacy shot, the one that becomes iconic, rather than the sheer Hollywood glamour. Think Elizabeth Taylor in her *Cat on a Hot Tin Roof* slip or Michael Jackson's famous *Ebony* cover, and you get what I mean—photographic moments that live on in history.

"Now, in my forties, and having enjoyed a lot of success, it's more about doing things for the greater good of everyone. *That's* the most important legacy there is. As well, life experiences such as losing my mother to breast cancer, losing friends to AIDS, working with visually impaired children for a film role, seeing friends who worked for fresh water in Africa and Habitat for Humanity—it all contributed to this decision. To asking myself, how can I take what I have and put it to good use?"

Thinking about brands and celebrities, I asked Bloch how he thought they can best partner with each other to do good work in the world. "There are two sides to that coin," he responded thoughtfully. "One side is how economically beneficial it is to the company; the other is who you get. Different people draw different crowds—Justin Bieber will be a bigger success than me! Judging it solely on a monetary value, the main ingredient is the amount of 'celebradom' for the celebrity. The other thing is finding the right match for the brand and, very importantly, finding a celebrity who's really genuine, who's good-natured, and not a pain in the ass. The biggest problem can sometimes be not the celebrity, but his or her management or agency teams and how they handle everybody, or worse, pillage the company.

"Again, you want a celebrity who is down to earth, cooperative, and not so removed from day-to-day living. Wendy Williams is a great example of that, as opposed to the type of celebrity who attends a charitable event but refuses photographs and interviews. Another one is Cee Lo Green (for Duracell), who I referred to earlier."

I remembered the story and it does indeed illustrate the perfect match between artist, cause and corporation. Cee Lo Green partnered with Duracell and the National Volunteer Fire Council for the Power Those Who Protect Us program, designed to donate batteries while supporting and raising awareness for our nation's volunteer firefighters. Cee Lo, it turns out, was a natural fit: his own mother had once been rescued from a near-fatal car accident by a group of volunteer firefighters  in Atlanta. Cee Lo tells his personal rescue story in the track *Thank You,* released as a free download on Duracell's Facebook page.

Bloch talked about choosing celebrities for purpose-inspired campaigns. "Some companies do it quietly, some loudly. Contrary to some people's opinions, it is not offensive to seek commercial gain from purpose-led initiatives. And, from the company's standpoint, 'Ms. Corporate America' can't be in charge of hiring. It has to be someone with intuition and a high level of compassion, not the person who's more interested in her latest Laboutins." This particular part of marketing, merchandising, and branding is, in the end, about one thing, he concluded: humanity. Purpose-driven people lead purpose-inspired campaigns.

For brands seeking to learn which celebrities are involved with what causes, they have only to check out Phillip's YouTube *Cause Celeb* clips, it's a veritable directory, a GPS for celebrities and their charities. Other great resources to reference for a detailed description of celebrity charity work includes Look to the Starts (www.looktothestars.org) and Black Gives Back (www.blackgivesback.com).

TAKEAWAYS

1. About brands and celebrities: how can they partner with each other to do good work in the world? There are two sides to that coin. One side is how economically beneficial it is to the company; the other is who you get. Different people draw different crowds. **Finding the right match for the brand is key** as is finding a celebrity who's really genuine, who's good-natured, and not difficult to work with.

2. Check the chart of leading celebrity-led cause initiatives serving multicultural audiences and global issues. Based on your brand's purpose, equity, and strategy to connect with the multicultural audience, some of these leading causes and campaigns may provide you with the **perfect opportunity to drive meaningful engagement** with your target.

3. There is huge opportunity to align your purpose with celebrities' "purpose" and "passion" to do good works. **Authenticity is vital** for multicultural consumers; the partnership and the relationships with stars must be built on real shared values. So, for brands looking to roll out purpose engagements and align with celebrities, be sure that the alignment/celebrity chosen has a natural passion and connection to the platform.

4. The old black and white scenario of win/lose, wealth/fame is fading, replaced by purpose and contribution. When you really care about your brand's purpose, when you are committed to improving life for others, you **engender long-term interest**—rather than fleeting curiosity—on the part of consumers.

Chapter 7

Align the Purpose of Your Brand with a Celebrity's Purpose

The purpose of life is a life of purpose. —Robert Byrne

Nelly Brings on the Bone Marrow Donors

When conscience arises, it's contagious and impacts the masses; it's no surprise that after Russell Simmons lit this match it grew into a flame. Other influential artists started showing up within their communities. As I share some of these stories, based upon your brand and it's purpose, perhaps one of these celebrities will be the perfect partner for you. Plenty  of other hip-hop celebrities are busy reaching out to the multicultural audience in various ways. Many of the hip-hop magnates are developing educational initiatives. They have turned into philanthro-capitalists, who create non-profit organizations for different causes.

When Grammy award–winning rapper and actor Nelly wanted to raise awareness about improving the quality of life for children born with developmental disabilities (with emphasis on Down syndrome and children born addicted to drugs), he founded 4sho4kids, which assists people by providing educational classes, and health care resources in the St. Louis metropolitan area.[1]

His *Jes Us 4 Jackie* campaign was started in March 2003 by Nelly and his sister Jackie Donahue after the latter was diagnosed with leukemia. The campaign attempted to educate African-Americans and other minorities about the need for bone marrow transplants, and to register more donors with the National Bone Marrow Registry. Donahue lost her battle with leukemia on March 24, 2005, almost two years after the campaign began, but her name lives on in *Jes Us 4 Jackie*, along with the possibility of saving lives through bone marrow donation. The *Jes Us 4 Jackie* movement registered some 1,760 African-Americans with the National Bone Marrow Registry.[2]

Will.i.am Hits the Books

Will.i.am of Black Eyed Peas explained on Oprah Winfrey's show that he set up the i.am Scholarship to provide future leaders and innovators with financial assistance for the entirety of their post-secondary education, along with professional opportunities at Dipdive.com upon completion of their studies. More than just financial aid, the will.i.am Scholarship is a vital investment in the future. For example, in 2011, the i.am Scholarship supported the inaugural class of i.am College Track high school seniors. College what? College Track: a holistic and comprehensive program, which nurtures both the academic and social/emotional growth of high school students to ensure each of them graduates prepared to succeed in college. "It's so great," enthused one of the scholarship recipients, "that he does something he loves and uses that to help others." Will.i.am's version of Homeland Security is an educated youth to be tomorrow's leaders.[3]

Jay-Z Takes a Stand on Water and Education

Jay-Z is another mega celebrity to take a stand on an issue, in his case clean water. That's right, water. Water for Life. Teaming up with the United Nations and MTV, he cited statistics that 1.1 billion people are living without clean drinking water, while 2.6 billion lack decent sanitation. Jay-Z (real name, Shawn Carter) had been looking for a way to help people and was struck by how many of the world's poor lacked such basic necessities. Having visited Africa, he stated, "As I started looking around and looking at ways that I could become helpful, it started as the first thing—water, something as simple as water." Jay-Z's efforts are not simply to expose the issues of water shortages and its effects on people throughout the world, but to help decrease the number of deaths of children who drink unsanitary water each year, and help communities build and secure their own water sanitation facilities, such as the very successful PlayPump program—a water pump that doubles as a Merry-Go-Round. Specifically, he has built one thousand such water pumps, saving thousands of lives in Africa.

Water isn't Jay-Z's only charitable project. In February 2012, he played Carnegie Hall in a glamorous fund-raiser ($500 to $2,500 a ticket, targeting large corporate sponsors) to raise millions for the United Way of New York City and the Shawn Carter Scholarship Foundation. "We're not just doing a show for the sake of it," said Jay-Z at a press conference. "For all these years, the Shawn Carter Scholarship Foundation has been really grassroots . . . Now . . . we're building this thing out."

Raised in Brooklyn's Marcy Projects, the rapper and his mom, Gloria, began his scholarship foundation in 2003 to help inner-city kids achieve their educational dreams. Since its inception, Jay-Z's foundation has provided 750 students with awards totaling more than $1.3 million.[4]

50 Cent and Street King Stand Tall

If clean water can fight disease, who's to say an energy drink can't take on hunger? That's the proposition offered by rapper 50 Cent, who is using Street King energy drink and leveraging the proceeds for meals for African

children in need. Every shot purchased provides one meal. And, for one week, every "like" he received on his Facebook page translated into a meal, too. Working in partnership with the UN's World Food Program, he hustled to get one million of those "likes," vowing to double his own donation to two million meals upon reaching that number. His goal is to provide a billion meals in Africa over five years. That, he observes appropriately, is what energy is all about. As of this writing, 50 Cent and Street King have donated 3.5 million meals through the program.[5]

Bill Gates Goes Back to School

Another program that we have had pleasure of partnering brands with is Get Schooled. Get Schooled is a national program that connects, inspires and mobilizes everyone from policymakers and corporate leaders to communities and kids as a way to discover effective solutions to the problems facing the U.S. education system. It provides resources and information, community outreach, and creative programming that engages a range of audiences to address America's education crisis. Get Schooled's co-developers are the Bill & Melinda Gates Foundation and Viacom, including BET Networks, MTV Networks, and Paramount Pictures. The initiative combines the foundation's deep knowledge of education reform with the power of Viacom's diverse brands to raise awareness about the challenges facing America's public education system, and provides information and solutions for students and their families.

One initiative paired Get Schooled with Bounty. Bounty, in partnership with The Get Schooled Foundation to help support teachers across the country, has provided teachers with the chance to get donations for the supplies that are most important for their classroom through a wish list on the website, Teacherwishlist.com. They're also doing this with the help of Grammy-winner Jennifer Hudson, Adrian Grenier of *Entourage,* and comedian George Lopez. These big names are contributing supplies to their favorite teachers from their school days, as well as to their former elementary schools.

Are our teachers really in need of such basics? A survey by Wakefield Research in 2011 found that 71 percent of elementary and middle-school teachers spend an average of $462 out of pocket per year on school supplies for their classrooms. Thus, teachers who registered their classroom wish lists on Teacher Wish List were entered for a chance to win a $462 grant from Bounty.[6]

Lady Gaga: Born This Way Foundation

International superstar Lady Gaga is currently the world's most popular pop singer and composer, recognized for her flamboyant, diverse, and outré contributions to the music industry through her fashion, performances, and music videos. Her achievements include five Grammy Awards and 13 MTV Video Music Awards. Lady Gaga rules on social media as well with 15 million Twitter followers, 40 million Facebook fans, and 1.6 billion video views on YouTube.

After seven years of musical success, Lady Gaga launched the Born This Way Foundation, inspired by a fan, Jamey Rodemeyer, who committed suicide after what his parents say were years of taunting because of his sexuality. The Born This Way Foundation was launched in February 2012 at Harvard University to foster a more accepting society, where differences are embraced and individuality is celebrated.

The Foundation is dedicated to creating a safe community that helps connect young people with the skills and opportunities they need to build a braver, kinder world. Gaga spoke to more than 1,100 students from several states, faculty, and invited guests at Harvard, urging the young audience to "challenge meanness and cruelty."

"This is not an anti-bullying foundation," said Gaga at the launch of BTW. "This is a youth-empowerment foundation."

Alicia Keys Fights AIDS

Eleven-time Grammy winner and actress Alicia Keys' pet cause is the well-known Keep A Child Alive (KCA), dedicated to caring for AIDS-afflicted children in Africa and India. Thanks to her heroic efforts as a Global Ambassador for KCA, and famous media initiatives—such as the star studded "I Am Africa" campaign featuring David Bowie, Iman, Gwyneth Paltrow, Richard Gere, Sarah Jessica Parker, Bono, and Lenny Kravitz, among others—KCA has been able to raise millions of dollars to care for young AIDS patients on both continents. Another dramatic highlight of this campaign occurred during Alicia's 2008 U.S. concert tour. That marked the debut of "Text ALIVE," where mobile phone users donated five dollars to KCA simply by texting the word "ALIVE" to 90999. KCA was the first charity to successfully implement an ongoing texting campaign in the U.S. Corporate sponsors for KCA include the likes of CBS, CHANEL, Clarins, Giorgio Armani, P&G Beauty, RED PR, Rolex, and many more![7]

With programs such as the multi-artist Buy Life t-shirt initiative and many more, KCA is a wonderful partner for brands looking to support global causes, raise awareness, and mobilize the multicultural community.

Ludacris and His Push on Education

Think of rapper Ludacris and what springs to mind? A Grammy award–winning artist, sure, a musician, an actor, but what else? How about The Ludacris Foundation (TLF) that he set up in 2000 as a non-profit organization to help youth help themselves? A commitment to giving back informs Ludacris' values and, with authenticity, transparency, and passion, TLF supports a variety of good causes that reflect his values while making a global impact. As a youngster himself, Chris "Ludacris" Bridges learned that the way forward is paved with seven things: spirituality, education, communication, leadership, goal setting, physical activity, and community service. Taking its programs to the streets, neighborhoods, and communities convincingly evidences the commitment of TLF. With three focus key areas: LudaCares, Leadership and Education, and Lifestyles, they're reaching youth at all age levels.

But it doesn't stop there. "Karma's World," a children's educational website inspired by Ludacris' young daughter of the same name, was launched to wide acclaim. With interactive features such as games, songs, stories, and lesson plans for parents, students, and teachers, the site also promotes social responsibility with a strong accent on education. Ludacris saw the opportunity for this enterprise when his daughter Karma expressed an interest in music and becoming "a singer like her daddy." Partnering with his own child helped him to teach her entrepreneurial abilities at the same time she focused on her education.

"Funky Bubble Land," "Wake Up Girls," and "Spacetacular Station" are but a few of the songs offered by the pint-sized artist. "We wanted the site to be educational, fun, and full of music that all kids will enjoy," said Ludacris, "but we also wanted it to teach kids more than just academics." Hence the additional emphasis on moral lessons, such as the importance of good manners, the rewards of hard work, and the idea that doing good for others brings good back to you, the definition of "karma." And, while little Karma Bridges performs all the songs, the easy-to-navigate site's creation came together as a result of Luda's own creative team and the feedback from focus groups comprised of teachers and children. Together they designed entertaining lesson plans about math, seasons and weather, gravity, the solar system, and ethical values regarding kindness, manners, and bullying. Future plans include teaming up Karma's World with The Ludacris Foundation to host contests and giveaways, not to mention releasing ten more songs over the next year, partnering with corporate sponsor Coca-Cola. Overall, the site is well on its way to accomplishing its goal: encouraging both kids and parents to have fun with teaching and learning, as well as instilling valuable business skills from a young age.[8]

DJ Beverly Bond Shows the World—Black Girls Rock!

Upon founding Black Girls Rock! (BGR), celebrity DJ Beverly Bond was on a mission that started as a t-shirt line to recognize Black beauty and has now grown to a cultural phenomenon. According to its mission statement, BGR is a:

> [N]on-profit youth empowerment and mentoring organization established to promote the arts for young women of color, as well as to encourage dialogue and analysis of the ways women of color are portrayed in the media.

This mission statement plays out in any number of exciting ways, especially when supported by celebrated headliners such as Tracee Ellis Ross, Regina King, Erykah Badu, and Tamar Braxton. BGR has successfully leveraged celebrity star power in tandem with a good cause to uplift African-American women of all ages. The sixth annual *Black Girls Rock! Awards Show,* held in 2011 at the historic Paradise Theater in the Bronx, was a celebration of Black girls who rock from the boardroom to the stage. As political activist and scholar Angela Davis said in a backstage interview at the BET BGR Backstage Rocks, "It's amazing to be a part of black women's lives, black women's dreams, black women's aspirations, and black women's accomplishments." BGR CEO and founder, DJ Beverly Bond, partnered with media influencers and community activists, including corporate sponsors Chevy, Target, and BET Networks for the gala event.

I recently had an opportunity to speak with Beverly about why she founded the organization.

"There are too many messages in the media that are too adult, one-sided, and objectify women," according to Bond. "I want young girls to know it's cool to be smart and creative and to be their own age." She cites 17-year-old actress Keke Palmer, star of Nickelodeon's *True Jackson, VP,* as a good age-appropriate contemporary for the girls. Speaking of her own role in the organization, and how it seemed divinely ordained, Bond remembers that, "I was a DJ and paying a lot of attention to messaging in music, videos, and media. Realizing how much inappropriate material was permeating the airwaves of our own communities, towards our own, I thought, 'what an injustice.' It was a conversation that lots of women were having. We noticed the way women who did speak up would get kind of tossed aside, their authenticity revoked with phrases like, 'you don't know anything about hip-hop, you just want to be a model in the video,' and that sort of derogatory thing.

"I realized our young girls don't know they matter because no one's telling them—especially in my area of music, in hip-hop, there was such an imbalance in terms of messages. Music after all is supposed to inspire you and make you feel good, to feed your soul, *not* to make you feel worse about who you are. Too often, in movies and TV shows, we Black women are just dismissed outright. We don't have a counterpart in the way that a White, Hispanic, or Asian-American woman is represented in the role of, say, wife. That has an effect on us as women."

When I asked her how her community organization aligned with celebrities' commitment to do good work in their own communities, she was equally vehement, offering examples of how celebrities have lent their voices to her initiative. "This is a conversation that resonates with all Black people, especially because we know what our community issues are: self-esteem issues that go all the way back to slavery and the way the world portrays us. This is what Black people know about! Thus, when celebrities heard about BGR, they wanted to get involved for that reason. For celebrities who deal with image as their primary job, it was easy for them to engage. For example, Regina King supported BGR in its early days, as did Carrie Washington, Tracy Ellis Ross, Mary J. Blige, Naomi Campbell, Bethann Hardison, and Queen Latifah—sometimes overriding their own agents and publicists because they understood its importance." She went on to include the opposite sex, stating that, "Men also supported our cause—Dennis Alba, Common, Anthony Hamilton, and others. This was significant because, early on, we couldn't pay any-one. However, because our cause was defined, it was authentic, and we knew exactly what our problems were, celebrities wanted to sign on."

Stressing the importance of a specifically defined cause, Bond added that being a celebrity alone is not enough. "Sometimes a celebrity will start a charity only to wonder why it doesn't get off the ground. You have to do the work first. If you're going to do cause-related work, it's imperative that you stand by it. Then you'll draw in the right kind of celebrity. You can't take on any celebrity, not without doing the research. Besides, you don't want to find out later that there are any skeletons in the closet."

I was curious as to what she looked for in her corporate partners. Bond said, "I look for someone who, first and foremost, understands our mission; someone who has done the research and who understands our work versus that of others; who understands the kind of tie you get with this type of brand. When people just want to buy into the hype of our TV show without buying into the rest of the work, that's a red flag. 'Star struck' doesn't have a place in our organization. People have to see beyond our celebrity popularity and sign on for the actual work."

Is there any particular BGR girl she feels particularly proud of? "A girl named Natanya. She was a very large, profoundly shy girl, a bullying victim, who I met while giving a talk at her school. Post-BGR, she is now one of the most outgoing, greatest girls in the program. The growth in her self-esteem and confidence is nothing less than amazing. As well," Bond concluded, "it's worth pointing out that many White parents with Black daughters have expressed their gratitude to BGR."

Looking to the Girl Scouts as an example of what her organization aspires to, Bond maintains that teaching girls about integrity, responsibility, and accountability—without assuming they know it already—is imperative in a world where too many negative messages unfairly impede the progress of young Black women.

The point I'm making is this: The trend of social responsibility is an opportunity area for brands. Many urban and pop culture artists have "passion" do-good projects that serve as amazing opportunities for a brand to partner with them in their efforts. Below, you'll find a chart of leading celebrity-led cause initiatives serving multicultural audiences and global issues. Based on your brand's purpose, equity, and strategy to connect with the multicultural audience, some of these leading causes and campaigns may provide you with the perfect opportunity to drive meaningful engagement with your target.

Celebrities Gone Good: Urban Influencers by Area of Focus

Urban Influencers Impacting **Education**	• i.am Scholarship Fund (will.i.am) • The Common Ground Foundation (Lonnie Rashid Lynn, Jr., "Common") • The Ludacris Foundation (Chris "Ludacris" Bridges) • New Look Foundation (Usher Raymond IV) • Susan Taylor National Cares Mentor Program • Magic Johnson Foundation • Historically Black Colleges (historic older organizations) • Thurgood Marshall Foundation (historic older organization) • Get Schooled Foundation • Dr. Donda West Foundation (Kanye West) • Zo's Fund For Life (Alonzo Mourning) • Shawn Carter Foundation (Jay-Z) • Will and Jada Smith Family Foundation • Make It Happen Foundation (Kevin Liles) • G-Unity •Tom Joyner Foundation • America's Promise Alliance (Collin Powell) • College Summit (Don Cheadle)
Urban Influencers Impacting **Arts & Culture**	• RUSH Philanthropic Arts Foundation (Danny Simmons, Russell Simmons; and Joseph "Rev. Run" Simmons, RUN-DMC) • The Kanye West Foundation • Bronx Charter School Art Auction (Swizz Beats) • Hispanic Foundation for the Arts
Urban Influencers **Empowering Women**	• Women's in Entertainment Empowerment Network • FFAWN (Mary J Blige) • Black Girls Rock! (DJ Beverly Bond) • The Tyra Banks TZONE Foundation • Hip Hop Sisters (MC Lyte)
Urban Influencers Encouraging **Financial Literacy**	• Get Your Money Right Financial Series (launched by Hip Hop Summit Action Network and Walmart Financial and later partnered with Chrysler Financial) • Manifest Your Destiny (Hill Harper)
Urban Culture **Going Green**	• The Campus Consciousness Tour (Aubrey "Drake" Graham) • Grind for the Green • Hip Hop Caucus Live Green Event (Black Eyed Peas, T.I., and Young Jeezy) • Project Água Limpa (Gisele Bündchen)

Hispanic Organizations	• Hispanic Heritage Foundation • Hispanic Scholarship Fund • Genesis Foundation
Urban Influencers Impacting **Politics and Civic Engagement**	• Hip Hop Summit Action Network • The Innocence Project • Latino Justice • Voto Latino (Rosario Dawson) • Boost Mobile Rock Corps • Show Me Campaign (John Legend) • Common Ground Foundation (Lonnie Rashid Lynn, Jr., "Common") • Community Engagement • Overtown Youth Center (Alonzo Mourning)
Urban Culture as **Global Humanitarians**	• Keep a Child Alive (Alicia Keys) • Yéle Haiti Foundation (Wyclef Jean) • Battle for Clean Water in Africa (Jay-Z) • Diamond Empowerment Fund (Russell Simmons) • DNA Foundation (Ashton Kutcher) • AIDS Foundation (Elton John) • Pies Descalzos (Shakira) • Steve Harvey Mentoring Program • Eva's Heroes (Eva Longria) • Believe Foundation (Rihanna)
LGBT Organizations	• The Trevor Project • GLAAD • True Colors Fund • Born This Way Foundation (Lady Gaga) • It Gets Better • Points Foundation

Meaningful Engagement

There is huge opportunity to align your brand purpose with celebrities' "purpose" and "passion" to do good works. This is a learning experience that I have continued to practice when working with brands. Authenticity is vital for multicultural consumers; the partnership and the relationships with stars must be built on real shared values. So, for brands looking to roll out purpose engagements and align with celebrities, be sure that the celebrity chosen has a natural passion and connection to the platform because those are the platforms that have yielded the most success. Continually do research to understand who cares about what. If you are currently working with a celebrity on an initiative, it is the perfect time to ask about what matters the most to him or her. You may uncover an opportunity to expand on an existing relationship with your celebrity spokesperson.

By now you recognize the difference between a celebrity just showing up for a one-off event and a celebrity who is committed to a purpose. It can't be stated often enough: When minority communities sense that your cause, and your brand, is authentic, they will trust you and show that trust with their patronage.

Celebrity Moms Lend a Cleaning Hand

Actress Julianne Moore was "thrilled" to roll up her sleeves and join Bounty to inaugurate the "We Love Our School Week" with parents and children in New York City. She acknowledged her concern for the cause as a mother herself. "What better way to show love this week than helping to improve your child's learning environment." Not to be outdone, Kimora Lee Simmons showed up at another New York City School ready to start cleaning. Joined by dozens of volunteers, Moore and Simmons demonstrated Bounty's commitment to provide clean, creative learning environments for schoolchildren across the country.

By now you can see how the old black and white scenario of win/lose, wealth/fame is fading, replaced by purpose and contribution. When you really care about your brand's purpose, when you are committed to improving life for others, you engender long-term interest—rather than fleeting curiosity—on the part of consumers.

As Tom Asacker, author of *Opportunity Screams*, puts it: "Are you strategically creating value, or are you pitching, broadcasting messages, and defending the status quo?" And I might add, who are you partnering with to make a difference? What exactly do they bring to the table? Julianne Moore and Kimora Lee Simmons are perfect examples of celebrities who do not just lend their names, they bring themselves and their commitment to the cause and get people involved, as the numbers show. They fit the spokesperson criteria in the following ways:

- Connected to message and strategy (education and schools)
- Appealed to moms 25 to 55 years old
- Are parents with children in school
- Have strong name recognition (E-score)
- Have current projects/newsworthiness/pop culture relevance
- Previous endorsements
- Number of followers on social media (Facebook/Twitter)

To wrap up the program, Kimora shared her inimitable "fabulosity" with a $50,000 dollar classroom makeover at the North St. Francois County High School in Bonne Terre, Missouri, the second school awarded such a deluxe makeover. The *Style* network star brought some sophisticated design back to her home state of Missouri and helped finish up another successful Bounty initiative, an initiative that acknowledged the lack of institutional resources in urban communities and found the right strategies in connecting cause with community with brand.

It was during the two school events that I realized celebrities that are truly passionate about your purpose are the best partners. In Harlem at Alain L. Locke Elementary, Kimora connected with so many of the students and with the passion of the principal, Susan Greene and I think she had as much if not more fun than the kids. Later, when we went back to her home state and unveiled the "Fabulous" Make Over classrooms, the gym was filled with excited students all wanting autographs. Anxious that she would miss her plane, I immediately started to think through the logistics and thought that only a few hundred would actually get autographs due to the time of returning flight. Present in the moment, Kimora Lee was not hearing it; she let the schedule go out the window, and spent the entire afternoon with high school students—

giving "fabulousity" advice, taking pictures, and ultimately signing *every* single autograph requested. As she finished, I noticed tears in her eyes, she was proud to come back home, she was proud to give back, and I had a feeling that she was connecting with yet another part of her purpose-inspired journey.

Factors to Review When Working with Celebrities

Relevance within your category

Does the celebrity resonate within your category? Ensure that it is a clear and easy association of why talent connects to your category or brand equity that you are bringing to life.

Connection to target

Take a step back and look at the audience your brand is trying to reach. Many consumer-oriented brands are focused on women ages 25 to 40, but that remains a broad group. Use research to understand your target audience, their interests, and the media they consume. Then determine how the brand could best use a celebrity to appeal to your target—or if the tactic would even work. Recognize that the use of a celebrity spokesperson is not right for every communications campaign or company.

Affinity for your project, brand, cause

Find someone who is organic to your brand and your message. Sometimes clients just want "a" celebrity, but it is important to look for "the" celebrity who makes the most sense for the brand. Consumers can find and share hordes of information about a celebrity with just a few mouse clicks, and they won't hesitate to call out relationships that seem inauthentic or contradictory to the celebrity's established personality. Tying a brand to a philanthropy can help secure a celebrity who might not be interested otherwise, and identifying with a cause they care about can allow celebrities to create stronger affinity with consumers—a win for everyone, including the philanthropy.

Newsworthy media

Understand if your celebrity is relevant within media. Also, has he or she been over-exposed lately. Will media care about his or her involvement with your project or campaign. Prior to signing the deal, it's okay to also do a soft sound pulse check with key media outlets.

Social media networks

Understand the celebrity's social media presence. How many people "like" a celebrity's Facebook page? How many folks are following him or her on Twitter? More importantly, how engaged are their networks; a million inactive followers does not hold great value. How much is the person being talked about on entertainment blogs and websites? There's no magic number, but the celebrity should be popular enough to justify the investment for your brand. If the celebrity doesn't have a Facebook page or a Twitter account, consider whether establishing one or providing other social media content as part of the relationship makes sense.

Current existing deals

Do a thorough background check of the prospective celebrity. Avoid unpleasant surprises by making sure a celebrity's past actions do not present a conflict for your brand. If your brand sells alcoholic beverages, for instance, check for DUIs or other drinking offenses.

How easy are they to work with?

This is really important for our firm when aligning celebrities with brands. At the end of the day, we want to ensure that the working relationship is enjoyable for all parties; the brand and the celebrity.

Notes

1. 4SHO4Kids: Husch Blackwell Sanders LLP, 190 Carondelet Plaza, Suite 600, St. Louis, MO 63105

2. http://marrow.org, or phone 800-627-7692

3. http://iamscholarship.dipdive.com, or through the Entertainment Industry Foundation, 1201 West 5th Street, Los Angeles, CA 90017

4. www.shawncartersf.com. Philanthropic opportunities and partnerships: info@shawncartersf.com.

5. thisis50.com, streetking.com; email infor@streetking.com; or telephone 855-753-6749.

6. getschooled.com, gatesfoundation.org, or telephone 206-709-3400 (Bill and Melinda Gates Foundation), or email media@gatesfoundation.org.

7. keepachildalive.org, email loshea@keepachildalive.org or phone (718) 965-1111. The U.S. address is 45 Main Street, Suite 720, Brooklyn, NY 11201.

8. www.theludacrisfoundation.org or contact President@theludacrisfoundation.org.

Chapter 8

Selecting the Right Community Partners for Your Brand

If we are together nothing is impossible. If we are divided all will fail.

—Winston Churchill

WHERE'S THE BEST PLACE to start in selecting the right community partner for your brand? After all, in the current environment, successful purpose-inspired campaigns require a fine balance. As purpose becomes more of a demand from consumers, we are seeing more initiatives, from Tide sending a mobile fleet of washers and dryers to areas hit by natural disasters to Pepsi Refresh giving away millions for ideas to improve the world.

As Scott Beaudoin points out in this regard, with a really well-defined purpose of a brand or company, what cause can do within that framework is help you socially express your purpose in a way that's delivering on a societal need. Societal need is where causes are born. Cause is always grounded in something that is a need within society. Purpose, as has been said before, can be expressed in so many different ways that it doesn't always have to be cause related. However, cause and community partners can expand your purpose initiative impact, which is why we want to dedicate a section of this book to serve as a guide when selecting partners.

Beaudoin goes on to say that consumers want companies to take on causes that are global in scope, yet relevant locally. Often, consumers feel that brands jump onto a cause bandwagon because it's easy, rather than really tackling the biggest societal issues facing kids *tomorrow*. The most important element in cause now is not appearing to be "me, too" or late to arrive. An excellent example of a global cause that has local relevance is bullying, and Secret's *Mean Stinks* illustrates the point perfectly.

Given that we know cause can be powerful if married to brand purpose, let's further examine guiding principles of how to identify the right cause to support and the right potential partners to bring your purpose to life.

Let's take a step back and review the process we have explored so far, and how we can further build upon the phases that have been discussed. In Chapter Two, I talked about the importance of Defining Your Brand Purpose, of really understanding how your brand fits into the lives of your consumers. Remember, I asked you to explore at a higher emotional and societal level as well, encouraging you to push past your brand benefit. By now, I expect you have a clear idea of why your brand exists and what is the soul of your brand purpose.

We then took a close look, in Chapter Four, at how that purpose fit into the lives of your consumers. You then went through a process of looking deeper within the life of your consumer to understand where your brand fits into the picture. The process describes a key phase in the MS&L Proprietary Four Phase Approach to Purpose—the Alignment Phase. This is the process that allows you to align your brand purpose with the issue or need in the life of your consumer. The graph below highlights the point of intersection between brand purpose and issue or need in your consumer's life. This point of intersection is the greatest area of opportunity for you to craft a purpose-driven consumer engagement platform. This point will give you a focused platform.

As noted, when you start to focus, it will be an opportunity for you to move carefully through the Alignment phase as outlined in the figure below. Decisions should not be made in silos, as you focus and set your objectives. Rather, use all the available information within your brand company structure. This includes:

- Internal interviews, employee feedback and briefing with key stakeholders.

- Setting clear objectives, audiences, vision, and goals regarding what you would like to accomplish with your purpose platform.

- Thinking about over-arching criteria in the development phase.

- Assessing deep consumer insight and analysis—not just traditional research but also, data gathered from your multicultural employees or multicultural internal employee networks.

- Review the needs of the issue that you are solving or planning to support. Social issue identification; existing or new issue direction. Your aim is to work through phase one in Chapters Two (Define Your Brand Purpose) and Four (Serve People and the World). After working through Phase 1, your goal is to walk away with a focused platform. Now moving to Phase 2 . . . (*see chart below*).

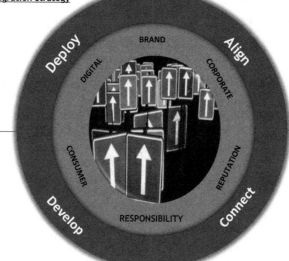

MSLGROUP *Beyond Purpose*™
Proprietary Phased Approach & Products

ACTIVATION PHASE

1. Influencer/Stakeholder Map
2. Online Engagement Strategy
3. Global Roll- Out/Implementation Plan
4. Tool-Kit for Regional Execution

DELIVERABLE: 18-36 Month Activation Plan & Migration Strategy

DISCOVERY PHASE

1. Purpose SWOT Analysis
2. Purpose Benchmarking & Best Practices
3. Partnerships & Programs Assessment
4. Communications Alignment

DELIVERABLE: Unique, credible and authentic "ways-in" to maximize purpose, inspire participation and drive profits

PLANNING PHASE

1. Communications Platform
2. Naming & Framing
3. Message Architecture
4. Partnership & Program Recommendations

DELIVERABLE: Platform, partners and programs that deliver on brand purpose and differentiate in the marketplace & category

CO-CREATION PHASE

1. Consumer Focus Groups
2. Global Network Concept Testing
3. Stakeholder Insights Report
4. Catalyst Community Idea Generation

DELIVERABLE: Big Ideas/ Concepts grounded in insights, universal truths, motivations & tensions

Deploy · BRAND · Align · DIGITAL · CORPORATE · CONSUMER · REPUTATION · Develop · RESPONSIBILITY · Connect

As we enter into this chapter's objective, i.e., selecting the right partner for your brand; look at Phase 2 of the above model – the development phase. In this phase, we will start to explore potential partners to bring your purpose platform to life. It's key that you have identified a platform unique to your brand; for Pepsi that was the focus of The Refresh Communities Project. Tide, for its Loads of Hope initiative, partners with the American Red Cross and Frigidaire. It's important, in this phase, that you take time to do a marketplace and competitive audit. Work with your internal and agency teams to conduct an ownablity analysis. Now that you have your "purpose-inspired" platform, there's an opportunity for you to identify a partner to bring your purpose to life. But why partner? What benefits does a partner bring?

- Third-party credibility among consumers

- Long-standing history of serving community or world

- Existing programs and reach within community

- Engaged influencers, community leaders, and thought leaders advocating for the issue or cause

As we get ready to examine potential partners, please note that there are different approaches to bringing your purpose platform to life, some of which include the following:

Approach 1: Finding the Right Cause and Community Partner

Vet potential cause partners and select a single partner to work with for your purposed-inspired platform. For example, this was approach taken with Hennessy when partnering with American for the Arts Association: Artistry Gives.

Approach 2: Consumers Select the Cause that Matters to Them

Create an infrastructure that opens the conversation to stakeholders and consumers to share with your brand what matters to them. Let consumers decide how your brand will support their community. This was the approach taken by the Pepsi Refresh Project, which allowed consumers to tell the brand which issues or community concerns they wanted to address. This was accomplished by Pepsi's website which invited online users to:

- Vote for your favorite ideas (find great ideas)

- Join a hot discussion (find your scene)

- Stop by Refresh stories (get inspired)

- Check out the Pepsi Challenge category (this month's challenge)

Thus, consumers could vote, join discussion groups, answer a challenge question, and share the latest news. And, if consumers had a "refreshing idea," they could learn about how to get funding. The project made ample use of social media to get people involved and proactively engaged.

Approach 3: Identify the three leading social issues facing multicultural consumers of the brand.

Consumers choose from the brand's leading social issues and determine which cause or issue they want to support. An example of this is being carried out by Subaru who, upon the sale of a new vehicle, offers buyers a $250 donation to one of five charities: Special Olympics, ASPCA, Make-a-Wish, American Forests, or Meals on Wheels. This has resulted in $15 million in charitable gifts in the last three years.

Approach 4: Brand creates a signature ownable purpose platform that is stand-alone. The program may work with partners to bring to life but the actual platform is stand-alone and *ownable* by the brand with or without partners.

Examples include Starbucks, who understands that purpose and profit are no longer mutually exclusive—they go hand in hand. Starbucks introduced the Green Project in 1985. Since then, it has offered a discount to those customers who bring in a reusable travel mug. It's just one of the ways it is fulfilling a commitment to environmental stewardship, working towards a long-term goal of 100 percent reusable or recyclable cups by 2015.

So, it stands to reason that either stand-alone *or* the right partner can lead to key campaign benefits that lend themselves to the movement of messages, product, and profit, and most importantly, people. According to the MS&L Group Social Activism Marketing Approach, when the mobilization of people occurs at the intersection of social responsibility and cause marketing, hyper-engaged customers, influencers, and communities spawn social movements. When this happens and is driven by a brand or company, desired business results are multiplied exponentially.

Factors to Consider in Selecting Partners

Over the past few years, Egami has had the opportunity to work with a number of brands on multiple approaches to bring to life their purpose platform. For those brands that choose to identify a leading partner to work with, and that are serving a multicultural community, here are some key factors:

National and Local Presence throughout U.S.

- Eighty-nine percent of African Americans and 90 percent of Hispanics agree with the statement, "companies that make sincere efforts to be part of the community deserve my loyalty." As Sabrina Thompson, co-founder of WEEN puts it, "Let's say a corporation gives a lot of money [to a cause], but to see someone in the neighborhood actually physically giving back, it stays with them [community members] longer—they remember it, and that's when you get that buy-in to the brand."[1]

Mechanism to address domestic and global issues

- Although global causes are important, for multicultural consumers, it's more important to address local issues at home. Remember: With local injustice running so high, it's important for issues to have local relevance, even for those that are global in a nature.[2]

Mission

- An organization's mission and existing programs must allow for both broad and narrow reach (national/mass activation and local city/grassroots activation).

History

- The organization should have a long-standing history of supporting issues of concern to multicultural communities.

- In order to leverage the credibility that comes with working with a long-standing partner, ensure that the organization is well known.

- If the organization is a newer organization, you may want to explore "owning" the purpose platform or partnering them with another organization with a long-standing history; (e.g., the approach we took with My Black is Beautiful, Black Girls Rock!, and the United Negro College Fund).

Partner Mission

- Organization's mission, supporters and founders resonate with multicultural consumers.

- Partner mission needs to be relevant to issues facing multicultural audiences today.

History of key influencers affiliated with organization

- The right partner with influencers can also provide a brand with influencers to drive WOM for their platform.

Opportunities for long-term partnership

- Once you have determined your approach and vetted potential partners, you also will have to vet them against your objectives. Here's an example of a vetting chart used to identify leading community partners for Hennessy's Artistry Gives.

2010 Artistry Cause Partner Recommendations

Organization	National	Local	Core Program Focus: Arts & Music Education	Target Audience Relevant	History of Supporting Multicultural Audiences	50 years or older?	Celebrity Affiliations	Chapters in Hennessy Artistry Markets	Ownable Program Opportunities for 21 and older
Americans For the Arts	✓	✓	Arts Education	Medium Resonance	✓	✓	✓	✓	✓
The Grammy Foundation	✓	✓	Music	High Resonance			✓	✓	✓
NAMM Foundation	✓	✓	Arts Education	Medium Resonance	✓			✓	✓

Now, once you have identified potential partners, it's crucial that you explore a true win/win/win model. Ideally, I like to find a model that provides the brand with a winning formula of meeting its objectives, the right community partner to serve its existing community and, a win for your consumers via a solution or platform that enriches their lives or the communities in which they live.

The ideal paradigm for effective partnership negotiation appears when both parties come to the table with a clear idea of what they want to get from each other, without the corporate partner seeking to undercut the community partner in any way. Everyone needs to feel their brand is being valued—that's a two-way street at all times. There also needs to be a real investment from both ends. Remember that 83 percent of consumers aged 18 to 24 *expect* the companies they do business with to support causes. At the same time, a healthy skepticism prevails, with 74 percent of consumers feeling that there is often "too much of a disconnect between the causes companies support and the brands/products they sell."[3] Therefore, speak the language of your consumer and adapt your messages accordingly. By having a winning formula, the partnership will feel more organic when brought to life via consumer interfacing, and seem more authentic when brought to consumers.

Here is an example of a winning model that we have used with brands and community partners. It's important that these models are analyzed in the early phase of partnership exploration to determine if a partnership is a match.

"Win/Win/Win Model"

What does each want?

Your Brand Here

What does each bring?

Consumer

Cause/Community Stakeholder

How does your consumer win?

Typically, a brand is looking to drive consumer engagement, build brand loyalty, engage consumers with purpose platform, raise awareness of the brand's role within the community, and focus on a long term platform rather than just one of a few engagements. The brand typically brings to the table name association of a trusted brand, resources/knowledge/insights, consumer knowledge, and marketing budget support.

Community stakeholders usually are seeking to advance their mission or cause, to touch and improve more lives with their mission, to add greater reach or support for programs and fund-raising, and to get their message out. What they bring to the table includes access to the target audience, credibility, programs, communication networks including database reach, and educational expertise.

Your consumers bring shopper loyalty, valued customer patronage, ability to refer through word of mouth, advocacy, and social media network. They desire a brand experience that adds value to their personal lives, shows up in their community, shares value with them, offers a way to get involved or personalize their involvement with your brand, and more.

One campaign that illustrates these points takes us back to the United Negro College Fund (UNCF). When it teamed with Verizon Wireless for Black History Month, creating a $5,000 dollar scholarship award for the best essay on how wireless communication has affected the world, all the right components were in place. Given that education is a leading issue in the multicultural community, the education platform resonates with Verizon's multicultural audience along with other leading issues facing their community. The key stakeholder, UNCF, brought to the table a long-standing history advocating for education, as well as credibility to connect with the multicultural community. It also had a wealth of assets with access to demographics, schools, and an extensive 300,000+ database to rally support. UNCF worked with Verizon to identify and target the types of schools they wanted, i.e., those with strong multicultural profiles and, as Monica Newman McCluney (UNCF National Director of Strategic Alliances and Corporate Relations) states, "created an entire marketing package that went to these high schools that included everything from fliers to web banners to messaging that they could use and games that tied back to the program."

Along with the scholarship, winners received a Verizon package with a state-of-the-art cell phone plus a year's worth of service. The program was, in McCluney's words, "wildly successful." Winners were announced in-store with the accompanying PR impact and nine times out of ten the entire family converted their service to Verizon. Verizon demonstrated its concern for consumers' education and thus validly partnered with UNCF's mission. UNCF provided the school and demographic information, Verizon the scholarship dollars. Win-Win-Win all the way down the line. Why? Because Verizon adopted that most crucial of all tactics: It sought to create a winning partnership that benefited not only its brand but also added value to its consumer and the community.

Another example of a great UNCF brand partnership that allows the brand to engage with another leading multicultural issue is the Empower ME/Wells Fargo Tour. Partnering with the historic UNCF, Wells Fargo provides a vehicle to understand what's important in life, i.e., education and financial literacy. Together, the UNCF and Wells Fargo created the amazing UNCF Empower Me Tour presented by Wells Fargo, showcasing celebrities such as actor Brian White, singer Kenny Lattimore, Toya, and more. Wells Fargo, in recognizing Black and Hispanic communities as being "underbanked" and in need of financial literacy, made a crucial connection with the UNCF to present a program that helps people understand how best to manage their money *and* access a college education, and acquire the tools needed to achieve that higher education goal. Promoting its career and college-readiness programs, the Tour focuses on middle school, high school, and college students, with interactive exhibits, college and career workshops, and panel discussions with well-known celebrities. Recent participants include Mo & Kita, Chef DAS, Alesha Renee, Flex Alexander, and Lamman Rucker.

Sensing a disconnect between young people and financial literacy, McCluney stresses that the UNCF estab-lished the Tour to address that dilemma, and encourage both academic excellence and fiscal responsibility. "Our member presidents realized that students were squandering their money away and graduating with debt. We leveraged our partnership with Wells Fargo and decided to travel around the country to address these needs on Historically Black College University (HBCU) campuses. The kids are excited about the celebrities, and the celebrities love giving back." No minds get wasted on the Tour, that's for certain; not with the huge, well-documented impact that celebrities (especially those from gritty backgrounds themselves) have on kids.

As you can see, the Empower Me Tour is a big win-win for both the UNCF and Wells Fargo. And it illustrates forcefully how purpose and cause build meaningful relationships between brands and consumers, as well as laying down the gauntlet for new brands to establish themselves in the Black community, where a healthy 75 percent of its members are brand loyal. A win-win-win scenario occurs when both entities enter the partnership comfortably and the corporation does not overwhelm its community partner. Only when corporations are transparent, when they value the community partner and are not just trying to leverage the brand name, is a successful new platform for brand loyalty created. As well, key considerations such as long-term commitment, integrated marketing partnerships, and overall consistency are vital. With something like the Empower Me Tour, not only does Wells Fargo attract thousands of new customers and influence change, but the UNCF, and young students and their families, benefit as well. That's what's called a win-win-win.

The UNCF worked closely with Wells Fargo on their banking presentation, which is all financial-literacy based, i.e., being able to attend college and manage your money along the way, without mortgaging the rest of your life in order to get there. Celebrities reinforce this message with a look at their own lives and what financial lessons they've had to learn, even while building their own brand and perhaps going from rags to riches. This kind of transparency resonates well with communities of color because it addresses their own lives, rather than just "sell, sell, sell." And it also demonstrates that financial literacy addresses, along with education, all other areas of life.

Other partnership guideline elements to be mindful of here include the key findings from EGAMI/MSL thought leader platform *Urban Works: Influencer 360*. In late 2011, Egami Consulting Group and MSL-GROUP hosted a four-part panel series with leading influencers in the areas of Community, Social Media/Digital, Culture, and Entertainment to discuss issues and trends that are relevant to the Urban Consumer.

Here are some takeaways and insights from that panel to keep in mind when building a partnership with a community partner:

Brands' commitment to community MUST be a sustained one.

Just as in personal relationships, long-term commitment is KEY. Urban audiences have a strong sense of responsibility and must see a sustained commitment from brands to improve the community and address issues within it. Social justice, domestic violence, economic environment, education, health, and safety were the issues most mentioned by Summit panelists. "As a brand," said Jenay Alejandro, associate manager of multicultural relations at Moët Hennessy USA, "it's important for our commitment to be long term and not just a one-off engagement."

Make an emotional connection.

Consumers, especially urban consumers, support causes for which they have an emotional connection. They tend to also gravitate towards *brands that show up within their community.*

- One-third of Hispanic and African American consumers report that they almost always choose brands that support causes they believe in, compared with just one in five Non-Hispanic Whites.

Be a physical not just financial, bridge between top and bottom.

A deeper commitment to the community is required and brands must go beyond financial assistance and establish a sustained physical presence within the community. The focus of this presence, according to the panelists, should be bridging the separation between top and bottom. "Undoubtedly, non-profit organizations need donations," according to Dupe Ajayi, External Affairs Manager at Taproot Foundation, "they probably always will. However, it has been proven that when professionals give of themselves on a consistent basis, it is more effective. Most non-profits need assistance by way of capacity building. Pro-bono service is THE new service." Think about the following:

- The Tide *Loads of Hope* program allowed employees to assist over 10,000 families in the New Orleans area with washing over 13,000 loads of laundry in the wake of Hurricane Katrina.

- The Taproot Foundation partners local professionals in accounting, finance, legal, web design, etc., with local organizations in need of *pro bono* services.

Stay committed.

- Brands must maintain a long-term relationship with the community and the cause, work to drive deeper levels of engagement, and commit to finding real solutions to the causes they champion when engaging in cause-marketing campaigns.

- The focus of the cause-marketing partnership should not be centered around just "writing a check" to the cause. It is no longer enough for brands to just place a sticker on a product to bring awareness to a social cause.

Striking the right balance between the entertainment factor, brand message, and the cause is key.

Both brands and causes must commit to a level of bilateral authenticity. According to panel members, this can achieved by staying true to core missions, values, and audiences while working together to achieve successful messaging on both ends. "I think there is an entertainment element," says Ellen Haddigan, Executive Vice President, RUSH Community Affairs, "that is part of looking at causes within urban communities."

- Chrysler partnered with the Hip Hop Summit Action Network for financial literacy awareness among urban youth. Both partners worked, as mentioned earlier, to find the balance between the artists' self-expression and language boundaries for the brand while remaining authentic on both ends.

Be transparent and authentic in your approach.

- Cause campaigns must be a truthful, sustained, and committed approach to improving the community and people's lives.

- The cause must closely associate with the company's brand attributes—"how does their commitment to this particular cause embody the inherent qualities of the brand?" A brand must be able to easily explain to consumers the connection between the brand and the cause, or consumers won't support it.

Clear campaign parameters are essential for success.

Brands must consider additional factors beyond partnering with a cause that resonates with their consumers. Panelists assert that brands need to develop clear parameters from the beginning that will account for resources, financing, authenticity and consistency with their brand messaging. "The most important way we choose a cause partner organization is where is the real issue, the real social need, because it needs to be authentic," states Katie McClue, Senior Vice President, MSL New York. "To be relevant, the cause community organizations need to be known in a positive way, they need to have good reach, and they need to have the resources. . . . They need someone on their side, just as we will have on our side to be the facilitator of this partnership." Consider these platforms and see if you don't agree:

- Diamond Empowerment Fund (DEF) reaches out to jewelry consumers in the U.S. to support African youth. The sale of the Green Bracelet helps support educational initiatives that develop and empower people in African nations where diamonds are a natural resource.

- Until There's A Cure Foundation raises funds and awareness about HIV/AIDS through the sale of The Bracelet and the money raised helps fund prevention education, care services, and vaccine development.

Cause campaigns must have BALANCE.

A purpose-driven campaign that aligns with a community partner must include all of these elements to be successful.

- Build strong partnerships
- Activate
- Leverage assets
- Acknowledge efforts
- Clear goals and measurements
- Communicate results and follow-up
- Engage employees/consumers while evolving

Remember employees are part of the community, too.

Panelists agree, brands have the opportunity to tap into their employee base as a source for cause ideas and talent. According to Dupe Ajayi: "If you are listening to what your team on the ground is doing day in and day out and what they care about, then you can definitely implement a successful program that will show that you not only care about the community. You also care about what your employees care about and the causes that they are passionate about. Think about this:

- More than 1,000 Paramount employees in 17 countries worldwide participate in Viacom's annual Viacommunity Day. Employees work within their community to paint schools, read to sick children, or serve the homeless. KaBOOM! has developed two successful corporate partnerships with The Home Depot and Dr Pepper Snapple Group (DPS). Under the *1,000 Playgrounds in 1,000 Days,* KaBOOM! and The Home Depot engaged over 100,000 employees to build 1,000 playgrounds.

Employees are your best asset.

- Employees should be a primary target for a cause initiative. When determining which causes a brand should support, companies should ask their employees what matters to them.

- Furthermore, employees want to work for companies who care about the causes they care about, and believe it's important for companies to match their individual giving.

Personalization is key among urban consumers.

According to panelists, causes need to feel personalized and must go beyond transactional practices (e.g., buying a brand that aligns with a cause). Social media can be leveraged to provide a platform that allows consumers to participate in the conversation. Nearly one in four African Americans (24 percent) Hispanics (23 percent) agree they keep going online because it's a way for their voices and opinions to be heard. "At the end of the day people want to feel significant," says Sabrina Thompson of WEEN, "We all want to be heard, we all want to be seen and don't want to be dismissed." Sabrina's thoughts are borne out well in the following:

- Pepsi Refresh project utilized social media to find people, businesses, and non-profits with ideas that will have a positive impact on their community. Pepsi invited people to post proposals for change in their communities and other users to vote on their ideas. Funds are awarded to the most popular proposals. In 2010, 7,000 projects garnered 51 million votes—287 ideas from 203 cities and 42 states won $11.7 million.

Personalization drives consumer support.

- People support what they build, therefore, brands must make consumers co-authors in the brand narrative. This demonstrates to consumers that a brand is listening and values what they care about.

- A marketing opportunity exists for brands, by using social media, to provide consumers with products or services that allow them to publicly express their belief in and support for causes that are important to them. Brands must acknowledge how sophisticated consumers are in their use of social technology and their desire to participate in meaningful change.

Design campaigns around Metrics and KPI that benefit both the partner and the brand.
(I will talk about measurement in more detail in future chapters . . .)

Let's look at another marketplace success story, the Kellogg's Share Your Breakfast campaign. This campaign invites consumers to share a photo or description of their breakfast. Each time a breakfast is "shared," Kellogg will donate money to increase school breakfast participation through Action for Healthy Kids. Part of the "Share Your Breakfast" success is that the process is simple, the cause is powerful, and the end result is huge and tangible.

Such a story goes far in showcasing accountability in one brand. But other brands are following suit. Why? While price and quality are still major factors driving consumers' purchasing decisions—and not just *what* to buy, but *from* whom—they still want more, especially from leading companies. And, in an ever-more digital world, they have the wherewithal to access more information than ever before. And say what you will, if a company is not accountable, consumers will gravitate toward the ones that are. They actively watch for evidence that companies live by their personal values and, conversely, notice when companies fail to practice what they preach.

Ethical Considerations

Ethics are something we hear talked about all the time. But where do ethical considerations really figure into purpose-driven marketing?

Corporate ethics take center stage when companies understand that Americans (when asked what a leading company means to them personally) relate more to companies that value corporate ethics. Being ethical (34 percent) edges out most innovative (29 percent) and most financially successful (25 percent) when asked the definition of a "leading company." Interestingly, women are more likely to value the leadership of ethical companies while men tend to respect the most innovative ones.[4]

Clearly, what is good for the public is good for business. And consumers are increasingly savvy about vetting corporate values. Companies signal their values to consumers in a multitude of ways, as we'll see in the next chapter. Meanwhile remember that, with more and more virtual contact going on, it is vital for companies to prove to people *who they are* in everything they say and do. Information dissemination to supporters must be a core component of CSR. After all, the majority of consumers expect to receive transparency and information in return for giving their support to issues and CSR programs. Thus, ethical trumps innovation, even *financial* success, as a top consideration for consumers. How will this affect your future decisions?

TAKEAWAYS

1. With a really well-defined purpose of a brand or company, what cause can do within that framework is help you **socially express your purpose** in a way that's delivering on a societal need. Societal need is where causes are born.

2. Purpose, as has been said before, can be expressed in so many different ways

that it doesn't always have to be cause related. However, cause/community partners can **expand your purpose initiative impact**.

3. Work with your internal and agency teams to **conduct an ownablity analysis**. Now that you have your "purpose inspired" platform focus, there's an opportunity for you to identify a partner to bring your purpose to life.

4. The ideal paradigm for effective partnership negotiation appears when both parties come to the table with a clear idea of what they want to get from each other, without the corporate partner seeking to undercut the community partner in any way. Everyone needs to feel their brand is being valued—that's a two-way street at all times. There also needs to be **a real investment from both ends**.

Notes

1. The Futures Company Multicultural Marketing Study 2009; Urban Influencer Panel Series, Yankelovich MONITOR Multicultural Study 2010.
2. 2011 MSL Group.
3. 2010 MSLGROUP Brand Values Survey.
4. MS&L Global Values Study.

Chapter 9

How to Leverage Social Media

@bigryanpark: things that help others is what get the most shares
—Ryan Park & Chris Brogan

SIXTY YEARS AGO, television revolutionized the way businesses communicated with their audiences; 15 years ago, the worldwide web did the same thing. Now, social media (along with internet video) has exploded onto the landscape. Facebook, Twitter, YouTube, and Pinterest are social media sites that have created major opportunities for businesses. These platforms are also powerful vehicles for brands to partner with consumers and causes to achieve social good and have led to the rise of social good campaigns. While 57 percent of blogging companies have earned customers from their blog, that percentage jumps to 92 percent if they blog more than once a day. Consider:

- Sixty-two percent of companies that are leveraging LinkedIn have earned customers from it.

- B2C companies have reported higher customer gains with Facebook, reported at 77 percent, while 65 percent of B2B companies have reported earning customers via their LinkedIn activity.

- Over 60 percent of companies leveraging internet for marketing have reported that social media has become significantly MORE important as a lead generating resource; over 50 percent of companies using offline sources like direct mail have stated they have become significantly *less* important as a lead source.

Facebook is currently on track to be the size of the world's third largest country, measuring its population in eight figures. That's right, *one billion* users. Having passed the $1 billion revenue mark some time ago, Facebook is now zeroing in on the next prize: one billion users. As the company claimed 800 million users in September 2011, it's no shock that membership of *one-seventh of humanity* is now within the behemoth social network's grasp. You've seen it, you've used it yourself, and you know how effectively digital social mobile (DSM) marketing programs offer content that attracts attention and encourages users to share it on their own social networks. As an addition to personal, small business, corporate, and non-profit organizations' integrated marketing communications plans, it penetrates areas that once were unreachable and has become a platform that is easily accessible to anyone with internet access, making active participants out of passive viewers. Not only do you open yourself up to a whole new audience, you can communicate and sell to your existing market, too.

Top 10 Social-networking Websites and Forums
by U.S. market share of visits, February 2012

Facebook	**62.9%**
YouTube	20.0
Twitter	1.56
Yahoo! Answers	1.00
Pinterest	1.00
LinkedIn	0.80
Tagged	0.68
Google+	0.47
MySpace	0.39
Yelp	0.36

Source: Experian Hitwise

As you may know, we call this engagement social media optimization (SMO) and it constitutes the best way to light a fire under any marketing campaign. In this chapter, we'll look at top strategies to leverage social media to drive engagement among multicultural consumers. We will also take a look at leading brands and campaigns that are on the forefront of practicing these strategies of consumer engagement, and take a glimpse into what marketers are saying about the trends that will drive the future of social media.

Purposeful online engagements can take a wide variety of forms, with online and offline components that range from contests to fund-raising drives and events that will benefit communities. With the rise of social media, most social good campaigns now include Facebook, Twitter, or other online community features.

Multicultural Consumers are Prime Targets for Social Media

Prior to looking at top strategies and trends to engage the multicultural audience, let's establish why this tool is a must when reaching multicultural audiences.

- Hispanics over index (263 percent) as viewers and as content creators in YouTube.

- A study by Pew Research shows that both African Americans and Hispanics over index in Twitter usage.

- A Forrester study also showed that Hispanics tend to over index in all types of social media.

- Pew Research projected that by 2012, 72 percent of African-Americans would be part of the online community along with 81 percent of Asian Americans and 71 percent of Hispanic Americans. Multicultural consumers' average online time per day exceeds 5.2 hours.

- Minorities (according to Nielsen) make up over 25 percent of Twitter and 22 percent of Facebook—this vehicle is part of multicultural consumers' everyday lives.

Currently, African Americans and Hispanics adopt smartphones at a much faster pace than the general population, with over 44 percent of

African Americans and almost 50 percent of Hispanics having smartphones. Chief among the primary usage of these smartphone devices is checking social networks. When 62 percent of Black and Hispanic consumers agree that social media influences their purchasing decisions, you want to, as digital strategist Michael Presson says, "Understand the peer community and the culture and atmosphere of your audience so that you are not only relatable, but personalized."

And, according to the Association of National Advertisers (ANA) website, "To reach multicultural consumers, more than half (56 percent) of marketers are increasing their investments in newer media platforms, according to an ANA member survey. Another 35 percent are holding their spending at the same level, while only nine percent are reducing their investments in newer media.

"The ANA's own website was noted most often (92 percent) as the newer media platform that *enjoyed the highest usage in targeting multicultural consumers.* In addition:

- Online ads on third-party websites garnered (80 percent)
- Search engine marketing, paid keyword (72 percent)
- Email marketing (70 percent)
- Search engine optimization, organic (64 percent)
- Mobile (59 percent)
- Social networks (59 percent)
- Viral videos (55 percent)
- Videos on demand (34 percent)

"Reaching audiences with targeted messages via different touch points is more important today than ever," said Bob Liodice, ANA President and CEO. "Particularly in targeting multicultural consumers, newer media platforms provide an effective way for meaningful engagement to occur."

In the survey, marketers assessed the effectiveness of newer media platforms in multicultural marketing as follows:

- Search engine marketing (cited as effective by 60 percent of respondents)

- Search engine optimization (58 percent)

- Firm's own website (54 percent)

- Video-on-demand (53 percent)

- Online ads on third-party websites (50 percent)

These numbers are easier to digest when you remember that, according to recent census figures, approximately 40 percent of the population under age 30 is classified as non-white, with minority groups representing the fastest growing slice of the U.S. population over the next half century. While companies adjust their product lines to satisfy this new population diversity, they also see the advantages of using multicultural marketing and PR tactics. Given this, it's easy to see why America's cultural diversity has such a big impact on the bottom line.

It's also important to remember that, according to Jessica Faye Carter in her online article, *8 Social Media Strategies to Engage Multicultural Consumers,* ". . . more companies than ever have begun using social media to reach multicultural consumers. If you're wondering what's behind the trend, it stems (in part) from a recognition of the size and economic clout of multicultural groups—now about *34% of the U.S. population, with an estimated spending power of over $2 trillion.*"[1]

And, culturally focused media outlets are also very influential. There is no greater proof of its influence than the $3 billion price tag that Viacom paid for ownership of BET in 2000. Indeed, the growth of culturally focused content and programming has skyrocketed in the past 20 years. So, do your research and know your audience. After all, according to a Pew study, 76 percent of Blacks and Hispanics expect the leading companies to use social media to connect consumers with others who share common interests. The opportunity for brands is to create compelling forums through which multicultural consumers can connect and share persuasive brand experiences, especially when Black and Hispanic consumers are twice as likely as their White counterparts to say they like being able to see other consumers' reactions and opinions about companies and brands in real time via social media.

For companies, multicultural social media campaigns deliver other benefits. Less costly than traditional marketing efforts, they permit comparative ease in updating and modifying strategies. The micro-targeting of particular sub-cultures within diverse communities allows companies to move beyond strategies targeting Blacks, Asian Americans, Latinos, or Native Americans generally, and specifically engage the sub-communities that exist within these groups, such as Africans, Brazilians, South Koreans, Indians, Puerto Ricans, or indigenous peoples.

With this in mind, let's look at strategies to explore when engaging multicultural consumers with purpose-inspired social media platforms.

Strategy 1: Culturally Relevant 365

First and foremost it's important to view your multicultural social media efforts, not as "one-off" initiatives, but as an integral part of your larger marketing strategies. As you create your over-arching marketing strategies, find ways to bring those efforts to life among various diverse segments (African American, Hispanic, Asian American, LGBT, and women).

Understanding how to tap into cultures within cultures online is key. Enlarge your comprehension of other cultures past the obvious earmarks such as language, music, and cuisine. From a good online article comes this advice, "Develop your niche cultural campaign knowing that there is a full cultural landscape from which you can draw inspiration and material for your social media site."

It's another axiom that, in an increasingly mixed-race society, consumers frequently navigate between (and within) different cultures. This is crucial for brands to know. Don't address consumers in one voice, or expect the same message to be appropriate to different groups at various stages of life. Generational differences impact how marketing messages are received.

Understanding how different cultures engage within various platforms is important to knowing which campaigns will most resonate across which platform. If you're a marketer looking for consumers from different cultures, one simple method is to visit social networks and blogs geared toward ethnic communities. Sites like MiGente (Hispanic and Latino cultures), Soompi (Korean and Asian cultures), and Black-Planet /AOL Black Voices (Black cultures) have substantial followers that appeal to advertisers. Microsites within larger, more popular sites like Facebook or LinkedIn provide further options, along with the websites of culturally focused organizations.

While you will find some different modes of behavior among various online cultural groups, most groups engage in similar behaviors—music downloading, information sharing and gathering, purchasing, and of course, using social media. The differences exist in the gray area where groups are using certain services, or different platforms to access the internet, a factor which could either limit or expand a site's service offerings. Organizations like AdAge, the Center for Hispanic Marketing Communication, Forrester, Nielsen, and Pew Internet (all of which are sources for this book) offer research specific to those multicultural users of social media. Breakdown of user demographics varies across social media sites, but that's ascribed more to the function of the type of site (e.g., media sharing versus connecting with other people), than to any hesitancy from users to interact across cultural divides.

Strategy 2: There is Value in Social Media with a Purpose

Leveraging social media to engage with multicultural consumers in purpose-inspired campaigns is powerful. Providing consumers a way to rally their social influence to make a difference is a key strategy that can be used to engage with purpose. Therefore, give them programs that allow them to have their voices heard to make a difference, to wear their community involvement as a badge of honor, and to unite their networks to get involved. Also, providing them with incentives that allow their social currency to be converted to real tangible support of their community is always a great idea. One example of a campaign that really speaks to the power of social media and purpose occurred

in March 2012. This campaign not only resonated among multicultural audiences but
also had wide mainstream appeal. Its name?
Kony. Its subject? Child soldiers. Its achievement? Legendary status in the world of viral
videos, with 50 million views in just over a
month on YouTube. According to data col-
lected by YouTube and reported by *The Los
Angeles Times,* the video was most popular
among teenage girls and boys aged 13 to 17
and young men aged 18 to 24.

That's all well and good, but Kony's important legacy is what it can
teach marketers about succeeding. For one thing, Kony received a surge
of attention in early March 2012 when a 30-minute documentary titled
Kony 2012 by film maker Jason Russell for the campaign group Invisible
Children, Inc., was released. The intention of the production was to draw
attention to Kony in an effort to increase United States involvement in
the issue of child soldiers. The video quickly received attention from
celebrities. Invisible Children hoped to raise Kony's notoriety enough
to provoke a massive overnight poster campaign, which took place on
April 20, 2012. It was a highly compelling video, featuring a sweet little
boy, to convey a simple, personal story about a complex subject matter. Also, the video used social media authentically and pertinently by
giving a call to action to viewers to spread the word. Then, it took it a
step further, asking viewers to help distribute the video through social
channels. And last but not least, the request was easy and plainspoken:
make the name Joseph Kony famous; help others to learn the name.
When asked, people responded by the thousands!

Yes, we can learn a lot from Invisible Children's *Kony 2012.* Despite
the heated controversy about this game-changing video's effectiveness
as a tool for significant change, there is absolutely no dispute about
its aptitude as a marketing phenomenon. So what vital lessons does
it impart to the rest of us? Again the answer can be seen as threefold.
Some of the core rules we can gather from Kony:

1. Define your uniqueness.

2. Construct a sound social network infrastructure.

3. Don't depend on social media (or traditional) alone.

It's not quite as simple as it sounds. Let's look at number one, Define Your Uniqueness. This means that, whenever you are creating content, do it in a way genuinely and clearly connected to your mission. Invest as much time as needed to deliver the goods in a way that engages consumers. Kony chose a little boy as spokesperson and the young voice explaining a complex matter through the eyes of a child was catchy and attention-getting. Who will you use?

Number two leads the way to the nitty-gritty of technology. Remember, Invisible Children had 54,120 Twitter followers prior to releasing the video. Who to engage and how to engage must be thoroughly researched before jumping the gun with content. That core audience must first be in place, as it is they who, when asked, will spread your message. And it can't be too easy. For example, Invisible Children identified key celebrities and policy makers with large online networks (people like Rihanna, Bill Gates, Katie Couric) and then requested their followers to Tweet at these people to share the video. Then, retweets from existing followers and famous people spread the word about *Kony 2012*. The result? A head-spinningly viral video.

Number three may sound counterintuitive, but it's true. The right online and traditional tactics are necessary for that important "viral momentum" to take hold, where growth takes place offline. Don't separate the two. Rather, remember that while social media drove the video among young people (13-to-24-year-olds), it was coverage of that phenomenon by radio, television, and plain old word of mouth that reached the older demographics. Hearing about it *offline* had the group aged 25 to 54 searching for the Kony video *online*. By reaffirming the core rules of successful marketing in an imaginative yet well-calculated fashion, it became a true game changer.

If you're now asking yourself, what about all the negative fall-out from that video? Good. My point here is not to defend its makers or its message, simply to examine what marketing factors were cemented in place to put it over the top. Take what you like and leave the rest. In my case, that means applying its lessons to any number of other marketing efforts. But take note: it's not by chance that what is being touted as the most successful viral campaign of all time was grounded in a purpose.

A second cause study that illustrates how you can leverage social media to engage consumers around heritage, culture and purpose is Verizon's Hispanic Heritage Month campaign. For Hispanic Heritage Month, Egami worked with Verizon Wireless North East multicultural teams to create a program that celebrated culture while leveraging technology to connect consumers across the nation with their family, communities, and heritage.

The Verizon Hispanic Heritage Hashtag Art included a live digital hashtag art piece, a montage, that consumers were able to access online. They could then add photos of themselves to the montage, and automatically become Facebook fans or Twitter followers at the same time. Clicking "Save Me" to the hashtag picture also gave them the opportunity to share with friends. Designed to target and engage with the tech-savvy Hispanic market, for every uploaded photo, HopeLine from Verizon donated $1 (up to $50,000) to Casa de Esperanza—a nonprofit organization working to end domestic violence in the Latino community.

Grounding the campaign with newscaster (and prominent Hispanic influencer) Soledad O'Brien, MSLGROUP/Egami not only leveraged Soledad's following, but also developed the strategic messaging behind the social media outreach within the wider Hispanic community. It's a perfect example of not only knowing your audience, but also where, what, and how they share. Given that, according to a Pew study, Hispanic cell phone owners are more likely than their White counterparts to access the Internet (40 percent vs. 34 percent), email (36 percent vs. 31 percent), or instant message (45 percent vs. 24 percent), the hashtag art mural provided the perfect tech-savvy modern solution that allowed these consumers to celebrate their heritage. Verizon achieved just that with the Hashtag Art campaign and its strategic philanthropy that focused on a single issue.

Social Media with Purpose Checklist

With the rise of online social media for social good, cause campaigns, I thought it would be helpful to insert the Network for Good Online Social Good Campaign Checklist. As you develop your social good strategies, these are a few essential questions to be examined:

Step 1: Cover the Basics

- Why develop a cause marketing campaign? What are your goals?

- How will the campaign affect charities and cause advocates?

- Who is the campaign audience and what action do you want them to take?

- Have you cultivated an online community?

- Can you sell the program inside your company?

Step 2: Frame the Campaign

- Can you communicate the social benefit?

- Can you link the social benefit to your brand or business offering?

- What campaign format will deliver the most social and business impact?

- Is your audience primed?

- Should you promote celebrity involvement?

Step 3: Get People to Act

- Should you provide incentives?

- Is it easy to participate?
- Have you created a sense of urgency?
- Are you inviting your audience to a conversation?
- Are you communicating with your audience where they are online?

Step 4: Build on Momentum

- Have you embedded a competitive element?
- Have you lowered the participation hurdle?
- Will you give interim rewards?
- Will you provide social proof?
- Can you tell your story?

Step 5: Be Prepared for Times of Disaster

- Can you flip the switch quickly?
- Have you addressed the response needs of your customers and employees?
- Do you offer a clear way to help?
- Can you communicate appropriately with customers and employees?
- Can you amplify the impact?

Strategy 3: Personalization is Key

Personalized content develops an authentic voice that connects community interests with relationship building. So go ahead and develop relevant messaging that engages and speaks to consumers as individuals, in the way they want to be reached and provide them with vehicles to express their personal views, sharing across their personal networks.

"Consumers go where they want to consume information," says Digital Strategist Michael Street of the MSLGROUP. "They want to know how a campaign speaks to them as an individual. Your target audience is always asking, 'what's in it for me?' So keep it clear and simple."

To that I would add my own observation that the trend is less technology related and more about personalization. This is no longer a push society, but more of a pull society. Also, social media provides brands with a direct route toward personalizing their names with consumers—giving your brand a distinct personality, while letting consumers know who you are and what you stand for.

So find your personality. Establish it. Show it off, whether you're a big brand, small business, or organization. Today, every company has both great customer service *and* personality within its reach. After all, it's been found that people everywhere desire human connection, especially in this world of automated call centers. Who doesn't want to be at the receiving end of a random act of kindness? That is what it feels like, when a human connection is established. And social media represents the marketing trifecta: fast, free, and ubiquitous.

Strategies of Two Luxury Brands

One company that illustrates this concept is luxury brand Burberry. It has proven that social media and luxury need not be mutually exclusive. Burberry covers the waterfront with its use of social media. Not only Facebook and Twitter, but its ubiquitous presence stretches all the way to the Chinese microblogging site, Sina Weibo. An early social media adaptor, quick to go where its customers were, Burberry's early use of the photo sharing app Instagram (flashing its new collection worldwide in an instant) was but one instance of it keeping one step ahead of the mainstream.

The high point of Burberry's social media use came in September 2011, when it debuted its 2012 collection on Twitter and Instagram just *before* it hit the runway. And the show was also streamed live on its YouTube channel. The results? Burberry's following has expanded to over 800,000 on Twitter and more than 11.6 million on Facebook.

The YouTube channel has garnered more than 12 million views. Not too shabby! And it certainly comes as no surprise that Burberry leads the way as the most followed luxury brand on Facebook. It is also the fashion brand with the most engagement, getting the most "likes" on its posts.

With Facebook launching its timeline for brands, can you guess who was one of the first to take advantage of this service? That's right: Burberry. It updated its profile with its company's illustrious history, going back all the way to the opening of its first store in Basingstoke in 1856. Its message for the rest of us seems to be fearlessness at breaking out of your comfort zone, to boldly try everything—no timid forays here—and then stick with what works. The last word goes to Burberry CEO Angela Ahredts. Attributing its meteoric growth to two main components, she said, "Our investment in flagship markets and digital technology has enabled our global teams to continue to drive customer engagement, enhance retail disciplines and improve operational effectiveness, further strengthening brand momentum."

Another venerable luxury brand to find functionality through social media is Mercedes-Benz. Its use of social media transcends mere marketing and giving its customers added functionality when they drive. You know how impossible it can be to find a parking spot? With a Tweet Fleet account, the Mercedes driver can do so with relative ease. The Tweet Fleet was introduced quietly, as befits the fact it was implemented in just one city and could be easily targeted to owners in just that city. It also illustrates how luxury brands can make use of social media beyond advertising, offering tools and functionality to their consumers and followers. Multicultural audiences are prime

targets for luxury brands as their increasing affluence demonstrates. There are approximately one million affluent African Americans earning a minimum income of $75,000 annually. Affluent African Americans control approximately $87.3 billion in purchasing power. The median household income for Asian Americans and Pacific Islanders is 28 percent higher than the U.S. average.

With all this market penetration, business ethics and transparency move into the forefront as never before. When customers want to know exactly what your company stands for, beyond the bottom line, social media comes into its own as the messenger. Now, when social media is constantly evolving and companies of all sizes are jumping on the bandwagon, it's crucial to do things right when using sites like Facebook, Twitter, and Pinterest for your business. With marketing in a universe where many consumers buy and sell among themselves, word of mouth is what drives the engine. For example, Pinterest allows people to bypass the middleman and go directly to the user, media, or artist. Bland, self-serving, and inflexible brands are incompatible with the public's expectations. But large or small, you can give great customer service and create an interesting and caring personality.

When customers know where to find you on apps like Foursquare or Facebook, they are perfectly positioned to pass the word to others and increase your popularity. Scared of putting a foot wrong in this brave new world? Don't be. A full 68 percent of consumers express more trust in reviews that include negative feedback, too. Flaws are okay with them. Believe it or not, that degree of openness can actually lead to growth in your brand sentiment, especially when people are using their mobile phones rather than computers for both browsing and interaction. In fact, phone usage is outnumbering computers five to one worldwide.[2]

Strategy 4: The Power of Tapping into Existing Communities

The lessons in luxury marketing apply across the board to all marketing efforts: Do the due diligence and connect to people who already care; connect to that valuable pre-existing audience. And remember that luxury market messaging is not about making new converts to a Burberry or a Mercedes-Benz. It's more about exciting the folks who *already care* about that particular market and inviting them to participate further.

Innumerable communities have formed and continue to form online, breeding like the proverbial rabbits. Some are professional networks, others focus on sports, lifestyle choices, fashion, entertainment, and a multitude of other subjects. When you find active communities that are sharing experiences and advice around the products and services you produce, then you have a golden opportunity to strategically reach them.

Strategy 5: Balancing the Online/Offline Experience is Still Important to Drive Connectivity

While technology becomes more and more integrated with our daily lives, it has yet to replace our need for in-person interaction amid the traditional bricks and mortar landscape. The challenge for marketers is to find the appropriate balance between online and offline channels *for their specific consumers.*

If you understand that faith-based communities are a great vehicle to connect with African Americans, finding platforms and influencers that provide access into that existing community is a way to engage the African-American audience. For a faith-based example, let's take a look at how P&G tied into the Gospel Superfest. The beauty of it is the way P&G integrated with a pre-existing audience. The challenge was to drive trial of P&G products (Swiffer, Mr. Clean, Bounty, Gain, and Charmin) while creating relationships with the African-American target to drive buzz and word-of-mouth. The approach? Leverage Gospel Superfest in Cincinnati as a platform to relay the benefits of the P&G family of products in a context that spoke to the target.

Mr. Clean on the red carpet with hosts Vivica Fox and Flex Alexander.

Among the objectives were:

- Generate on-site trial and relay product benefit messaging.

- Activate community interest through African-American media.

- Onsite activations included:

  - The Mr. Clean team created an experiential bathroom on-site to drive awareness of Mr. Clean's new superior cleaning and fresh scent products.

  - The Bounty brand created the Bounty Soul Food Cook-off and used B. Smith as the event hostess and spokesperson alongside three Gospel choirs.

The results were spectacular as the campaign achieved more than 79 million media impressions including the *Yolanda Adams Morning Show,* the *Tom Joyner Morning Show,* and *AOL Black Voices with Jawn Murray.*

It's crucial to keep in mind when reaching and tapping into existing communities that it's not about reaching everyone but rather, to drive meaningful engagement within that community. Remember that one percent is a win, according to marketing executive Troy Brown, founder and CEO of one50one LLC. One percent of Facebook equals 70 million people! And, as Brown suggests, what the brand must do is tie into an already densely populated target community. You will note that the Gospel Fest community activation was an offline event. However, it was still viewed as a powerful vehicle to build online communities. How? It was mining within an existing strong multicultural community network. It could leverage those activations to strategically invite this audience into its online communities.

Too often companies focus on building up DSM without focusing on connectivity. For example, you may need to integrate mobile for more robust messaging and integrate relationships that way. It's crucial when building up DSM platforms to consider all the places that your consumers may be and provide them with an equally robust experience, no matter their choice of platform.

If you don't, consumers sense that you don't understand them. Smartphone, as Troy Brown says, is still only 33 percent of the cell phone market. What are you doing for people with other phones—what kind of mobile web experience are you providing them? Your website has to be designed for the mobile web in order to offer the same experience to the end user, be they on the computer, tablet, or cell phone, or some other device as yet unknown.

Strategy 6: Be Willing to Lose a Little Control

Also, while it may sound counterintuitive, be willing to lose a little control. Put your message out there and let go. Let the users take over. After all, DSM is social. You can't possibly control every aspect of it. Don't be afraid to allow people to get in there and mix it up because that's how other people get passionate about the thing you already care deeply about.

Use DSM not to change people's minds, but to connect to a group of like-minded people and let those people drive the change. As we look at cause or purpose-driven responsibility, the job of DSM is to raise the call to drive awareness to an issue, financial contributions, and volunteering, not in a static Facebook way, but in a way that makes people aware of the cause and thus excites the base. Then, allow them to motivate their friends. Tap into what's already there, run parallel, and fold your message in. And, as Tim Johnson, Director of Social Media at one50one, LLC adds, if you're doing a cause, make it about the cause or greater purpose. A brand has to be willing to forfeit some of its own coverage for the cause itself. As people engage on deeper levels, you can rest assured they'll come into contact with the brand. Just provide infrastructure, support, and be ready as more people become involved. Says Johnson: "Just because you're not at the front door doesn't mean you don't get to furnish the house."

Think back to Kony. Kony tapped into pre-existing communities and brought together a lot of collaboration; and connected to people with the highest social capital to get them involved. That was the major difference: A whole lot of people came together and brought their following along with a clear call to action. Those are lessons brands need to learn: Clear call to action, low effort, and placed before a pre-existing community.

Strategy 7: Understanding Who's Got Klout

We all know what clout means, but now there's Klout, a new internet service whose mission is to provide insights into everyone's influence. Measuring your influence based on your ability to drive action in social networks, Klout processes this data on a daily basis to give you an updated Klout Score each morning. Here are a few of the actions they use to measure influence:

- Twitter: Retweets and Mentions

- Facebook: Comments, Wall-Posts, Likes

- LinkedIn: Comments, Likes

- Foursquare: Tips, To-Do's, Done

- Google+: Comments, Reshares, +1

Other networks that they're working to measure are Facebook Pages, YouTube, Instagram, Tumblr, Blogger, Wordpress, Last.fm, and Flickr. You can already link these accounts with your Klout profile, and Klout will soon be able to incorporate your activity from these networks to their score.

What about the type of influencers who are most effective at activating the multicultural community around a cause, i.e., those who understand which influencers have online clout/influence? We will focus more on this in the next chapter but it's key when devising social media strategies that your social media influencers have the ability to drive real engagement and actions. The power of DSM resonates across all brands. When a particular consumer segment sees someone to identify with, something to aspire to have, there's always going to be a conduit there to engage with the customers. It's considered much more effective to engage with the multicultural consumer segment via individual social mobile channels because of over-indexing and because of the way they use devices that general market consumers don't. Here are two examples of barrier-breaking influencers with mega social media Klout:

Soulja Boy

Rap artist DeAndre Cortez Way, better know as Soulja Boy, has become a highly sought-after authority on social media engagement after using the power of social media to self-publish his single, *Crank That (Soulja Boy)* on the internet. It eventually became number one for seven non-consecutive weeks and his debut studio album, *Souljaboytellem.com*, was certified platinum. Soulja Boy has been listed at #18 on the *Forbes* list of Hip Hop Cash Kings of 2010 earning $7 million that year, a career that started on the internet via social media, and; he is only 22 years old.

Lady Gaga

Stefani Joanne Angelina Germanotta, better known as Lady Gaga, has amassed a social media following that makes her one of the most popular global musical icons. With over 2.1 billion combined views of all her videos online, Lady Gaga has over 47 million "likes" on Facebook and is #1 on Twitter with over 25 million followers and over 20 million Google+ followers. Her third studio album, *Born This Way*, broke the iTunes record for the fastest rise to the # 1 on release day. She was named one of *Forbes's* Most Powerful Woman in the World in 2011 and was included in *Time's* annual "The 2010 Time 100" list of the most influential people in the world.

Strategy 8: Original Content is Key

Platforms that tap into communities to provide original content win along with brands that have a constant flow of original and unique content to keep their audience engaged.

The Future of Social Media—Trends to Keep Top-of-Mind

As you think of crafting your purpose-inspired initiatives, some of the top media trends to bear in mind are the following.

Social Shopping Experiences

As we saw with Burberry, DSM is the new shopping exchange. The social platform that is fashion focused is a watch-worthy trend. Changing the way consumers shop, discover products, and make wardrobe decisions, this kind of platform is a perfect storm of community, content, and commerce.

Many Faces of TV

Everything old is new again and the latest screen culture marks a nostalgic comeback. Tablets and Smartphones are poised to be the new screen experience, making social TV the new certainty. The difference is in the interaction component that permits users to share their experiences, creating a two-way street from a one-way.

Doing Good

Crowdsourcing may not be new but the past year has clearly demonstrated that allowing others to make content is a surefire go. The future will bring new and meaningful forms of DSM crowdsourcing that drives community efforts to improve the world.

Gaming is Social

With browser gaming in, downloading games is officially out. The social gaming arena is reaching a boiling point, and the switch to browsers (for convenience) and more gratifying gameplay experience is sure to entice new demographics.

Engagement

The biggest change we'll see is developments made within existing networks, and perhaps even the development of new networks alto-gether as integration is so achievable. But here's the thing: Conversa-tions have to be initiated (as opposed to continued) in the mobile space. Look forward in the near future to being just as engaged on your cell phone as you are on your computer or tablet. Engage-ment is the big trend right now, across all platforms. As marketing expert Troy Brown says, "Fifty percent of Hispanic traffic comes from mobile devices. When Facebook says we have to rewrite Facebook to be more mobile friendly, that should tell you something."

Crowdmoving

The top trends marketers should keep in mind as they reflect upon engaging multicultural audiences using DSM can be expressed in a single question: who's moving the crowd? That's the alpha and the omega. Brands have to weave themselves into the right narrative, e.g., a breast cancer survivor telling her story through the Susan G. Komen Foundation. The growing segment in content and consumption right now is mobile video, especially with the multicultural audience. When professional-looking films can be made on an iPhone, that playing field is leveled even further. Consider the example of blogger "Madbury," a jock at Rutgers University who has Adidas and Nike following him. The former even flew Madbury and his team over to Germany to discuss how best to leverage DSM worldwide and partner with him. Not too shabby for a youngster still in college.

Stories like that will always, as the old saying goes, sell newspa-pers, but what about actual measurement factors when gauging the success ROI of your own programs? There are four areas:

- Growth (i.e., how many Facebook and Twitter fans?)
- Presence (i.e., where do we exist in the conversation?)
- Content
- Ratio of positive versus negative comments

These factors are all key to the foundation of what DSM is. It turns on relationship measures, the results of all the polls, and rewards those folks who have interacted the most over all platforms. In other words, return on engagement.

TAKEAWAYS

1. Facebook, Twitter, YouTube and Pinterest are **social media sites that have created major opportunities for businesses**. These platforms are also powerful vehicles for brands to partner with consumers and causes to achieve social good and have led to the rise of social good campaigns.

2. America's cultural diversity has a big impact on the bottom line, and more companies than ever have begun **using social media to reach multicultural consumers.**

3. Leveraging social media to engage with multicultural consumers in purpose-inspired campaigns is powerful. Providing consumers a way to rally their social influence to make a difference is a strategy that can be used to engage with purpose. Therefore, **give them programs that allow them to have their voices heard** to make a difference, to wear their community involvement as a badge of honor, and to unite their networks to get involved.

Notes

1. http://mashable.com/2010/04/21/social-media-multicultural/
2. Genconnect.com

Chapter 10

The Importance of Influencers

He who influences the thoughts of his times, influences all the times that follow.

—anonymous

Influencer Networks Are Crucial

PUBLIC RELATIONS, which we will cover in the next chapter, has always been about creating and enhancing connections, and never more so than in this era of social media. However, closely allied with a public relations effort are influencers that are among a brand's most valued connections.

The process of using relationships with influential people that leads to assisting you in creating visibility for your product or service is known as influencer marketing. This type of marketing rides on the prospect of something fabulous for your potential customers, along with the audience of the influencer. It also depends on one other element—the great relationship you build with the influencer. Basically, influencer marketing means marketing to people who most influence the sales decision, rather than to the end customer. In a nutshell, your marketing has to target both the person with the credit card *and* the people who affect whether or not he or she uses that credit card. No matter who the influencer is—celebrity or friends and family—influencers often have a larger audience than your brand does, or at the very least, a different audience.

However, the benefit is much larger than that. Let's say you had 100 followers in your Twitter account that shared a piece of content, and this results in 20,000 people seeing what they shared. This may result in 20 additional shares and 10 links.

Now consider the same audience being reached by one influencer. Those 20,000 connections will be much more responsive to the shared content because of the trust they have in the opinions of the influencer, and this might result in 100 additional shares and 50 links.

That's a pretty hefty advantage. Further, the search engines actively calculate author authority, so they will also place more weight on the vote of the influencer.

Leveraging the Influencer

There are many ways you can engage with influencers but first and foremost it's key to build an authentic relationship with them. Identify those influencers that have interest in your brand. The brand-influencer relationship can take many different forms. Imagine influencers:

- Serving as a brand ambassador or an on-going brand correspondent, covering important moments in time for your brand;

- Co-creating content with your brand for social media channels;

- Writing a blog post or article about you; posting on their channels as well as yours;

- Sharing information about you in their social media accounts; note it's critical that this is done in their own voice and not simply as paid placement/brand messaging;

- Asking or permitting you to guest post on their site.

The list goes on and on. You can be creative in the relationships you craft but remember that influencer marketing is about your "relationships" and "influence."

Good marketing and public relations involve far more than mere list making of your top influencers. Don't get me wrong—metrics and scores are indeed valued. Examined from the perspective of topical relevancy, they can do a great job of identifying potential influencers and help you to determine the focus of the majority of your efforts. But good marketers need to dig a little deeper than the simple number. We can't assume that any magic bullet (no matter how well engineered) can solve all of our challenges.

You've got to recognize what your influencers care about. How to do this? Explore their previous blog posts and articles. Peruse their clip files. See where they've been cited and interviewed. What are they talking about? What are they saying? What were they interested in last month? What do they care about this week? What's happening today that's relevant to them?

That's the point where you move beyond generic communications, where you begin to build relationships and create personal pitches that are far more likely to resonate with your influencer and garner your desired response. Working with influencers can be hugely advantageous in marketing—but it's essential to be smart about it.

Internally, we thought it would be cool to identify our top multicultural influencers by category. For some key influencers to keep top of mind, download our Multicultural Influencer list—based on product, service, and/or brand—at www.egamiconsulting.com/influencerlist. Remember, for brands looking to engage, it's all about relationships.

* * *

A Day in the Life of an INFLUENCER
Brands Understand Her Power: Bevy Smith

From hip publications like *Vibe* and *Rolling Stone* to brand partners such as Range Rover, if it's chic, sexy, and up-to-the-minute, it's likely that Bevy Smith has a placed her "influential" stamp on it. A writer, television personality, hostess, socialite, and the creator of *Dinner With Bevy,* the inimitable Bevy Smith has done it all. The brands she has worked with include Target, Belvedere vodka, Hugo Boss, My Black Is Beautiful, and Alberto Culver. To explore the essentials

of a great influencer-brand relationship, I knew this outspoken New York socialite would add great value to the conversation. I was delighted when she agreed to take time out from her hectic schedule to meet with me for an interview.

Behind every Great Woman Lies a Great Purpose

So how did Bevy Smith get her start? She began her career many years ago as a receptionist at the Peter Rogers Associates advertising agency. Always careful, even then, to go the extra mile, Smith stood out in this humble job as a well-dressed, well-spoken, and well-read employee who never wasted time. The people in power took notice, and when her mentor, Jeff McKay, left to form his own agency, she went with him. There she learned about client relationships and ultimately became media director, a position that landed her working with *Vanity Fair*, with legendary designer Bill Blass, and attending all the fashion collections.

This young lady from Harlem went from reception to covering every major fashion season, including shows in Milan and Paris. Sounds thrilling to me, but eventually Smith grew bored. Passing by an opportunity to sell advertising at *Essence*, she instead took a chance on the hip-hop *Vibe* magazine, a place seemingly at odds with her upscale fashion background. However, she carved out her role, with the intention of bringing haute couture into the world of hip-hop and urban culture.

But guess what? The job turned out to be Milan and Paris couture; she became the connector among luxury, fashion, and urban culture. Bevy was once again riding the crest of the wave, this time internationally. When she left *Vibe,* many of her loyal fashion brands followed Smith when she transitioned to *Rolling Stone*. Bevy interviewed with *Rolling Stone* in hopes of expanding her opportunities to do work on the editorial side, having been recommended to the magazine by the vice-president at Louis Vuitton.

"I didn't even bring a resume to the interview. I just told them to tell me what brands they wanted in the magazine and offered them the phone numbers for the VPs of every brand they named. That said a lot more than any resume!" Her powerful relationships sealed the deal and

Smith found herself *Rolling Stone*'s senior fashion editor, *and* the only Black person there.

By the time she left, only ten months later, fashion advertising was up 30 percent! So why leave? "All the way back at *Vibe* I was itching for a new life. After *Rolling Stone*, I took a three-month sabbatical in South America, Africa, and Costa Rica. I was reading the books *The Four Agreements* and *The Artist's Way*, and listening to Jay-Z's *Black Album*. Those were the three ingredients to help me get my focus together. I also took DJ classes and photography classes, as well as acting lessons. I was 38 years old and changing my game. I stepped out on faith, you see, and God did the rest.

"Then Mimi Valdez, editor-in-chief at *Vibe,* called and asked me to come back. Once again, the commonality within this purpose-led journey, whether you are person, entrepreneur, or brand, is proven. It takes some soul searching, some internal and external conversations to find your authentic voice, service, product, and offering to the world. Valdez asked me to be fashion editor-at-large, name on the masthead, but not have to go in. So, by saying yes to the opportunity, I broke all the rules and created my own! I had an advice column in *Vibe* called "Bevy Says," and I've still retained that brand. I did *Vibe*'s Style column where I took one fashion item and told readers how to wear it and where to go in it. And I also worked with celebrities." Smith tied celebrities and designer brands together to encourage the brands to buy advertising.

"Being *Vibe*'s editor-at-large is what got me onto TV," Smith explained. "When VH1 or BET needed someone to comment on fashion or style, they called me. It was crazy the way it all came together. It was far too magical to be about just me being fabulous, you know? It was God at work."

I asked Bevy to define her brand purpose. "My brand purpose is to motivate and to mentor, and to lead as an example. I take being a role model very seriously. I'm very clear on that. I know that there are a lot of young women watching my movements and I don't want to set a bad example for them. There are certain things," she emphasized, "that I will not do because it would not only violate my brand tenets but the way I was raised." Smith acknowledged that she has a commitment to

Harlem, where she grew up, and its residents. She stays in Harlem, she said, because she knows she is a role model for the youth there.

"I knew the kids in my building were looking at me. I was a role model for them. They'd see me in the magazine. Now that I'm on TV, multiply that number of kids and I'm a role model for all of them, too. As far as being authentic, my community is amazing and I never felt I had to run away from it or put on airs. Where I'm from is already fabulous. There's such legacy attached to it. African Americans *move* pop culture in this country and therefore in the world. We want what's new and hot."

Given all that, I wondered what advice she would give small business owners or entrepreneurs who are trying to define their brand purpose. A brand has to have integrity and a calling card and a life attached to it, Smith maintained. "Your brand is just an extension of you. You have to know what you're comfortable with for your own personal life and then that has to be an offshoot into your brand."

Smith flipped trendsetting on its head. She took real-life insights back to the brand. "The people of the Harlem Renaissance were decked out to the nines. And this is who we are; this is our heritage. Urban culture is not going back to t-shirts and jeans. We come from a culture who take pride in their appearance because they *had* to work extra hard at it, historically, because of their race in a white country. We had to fight against stereotypes. So when people wonder why we over-index in fragrance, in cosmetics, in fashion, that's why. It's in our background. That's why I always emphasize to kids who are interested in marketing that they have to know history. If you're dealing with the African-American market, you have to know history."

Bevy the Influencer

Smith said she established herself as an influencer at age 13, but that the advent of social media was a game changer for her. While Facebook gave her the ability to have conversations with many people at one time, Twitter really changed her role as an influencer.

"Twitter changed my life. It coincided with Oprah's retirement when, on that last show, she said that we all have a platform. I realized then I had to take Twitter seriously. I already had 10,000 to 15,000 followers but I didn't see it as my platform. I do now. When people ask me about when I'll have my own TV show, I say I have it. I have it *every day*, from 9 am to 12 pm, on Twitter. It's a form of talk show where I'm bringing up topics and *engaging* people and connected. It's great for my brand. And it moves the needle, rather than a single one-off tweet." Now, with over 39,000 Twitter followers, her influence continues to grow.

The Brand-Influencer Relationship

Bloggers and influencers are becoming the new celebrities. I asked Smith what makes an authentic influencer-brand partnership? "For one thing," she answered thoughtfully, "you have to believe that the person is really connected and you can tell that through their messaging. I'm not paid every day to talk about Belvedere vodka but when I go out, if I'm having vodka, it will be Belvedere. It will just naturally be a part of my conversation. I like the way it's not artificially flavored. I know that because I work with them and so I like it and I drink it. It becomes natural; it's a real connection. It's organic. Also, if you're doing a charity event with a celebrity, he or she should know that you will work with them in a variety of aspects to provide deeper engagement. I never do exactly what's on the contract; I always go above and beyond."

What she particularly seeks in brand partners is for them to be a good marquee brand. Luxury and quality are the *core* of her own brand. Marketers, she warned, have to be careful not to have their heads turned by any one particular celebrity, or any one piece of music.

I asked, "What are the best channels and mediums to leverage relationships with consumers? What are the best ways for brands to work with influencers?"

Her answer, like the question, was twofold. "Number one, I love events," she said, "because I really love to touch people, so the work that we did with My Black Is Beautiful during Essence Music Festival was really great for me because I had a chance to talk with the consumers as a girlfriend, which is how they think of me anyway. Number two,

I also love social media. You have so many people converging at once and then there's the re-Tweet factor when you have a message that really resonates and there's no telling how many re-Tweets that message can actually get. So I like events, I like social media. PR is only as good as the social media that carries it, because just having it in one space doesn't work. There are way too many options now. People are not just locked onto one thing. Once upon a time you either read the *Wall Street Journal* or the *New York Times*. Now, you read much more online, plus a gazillion websites that you tap into. So, PR without social media incorporated into it misses the boat."

When I asked her about the best ways for brands to partner with celebrities to do good works, she was explicit. "One of the best ways to leverage celebrities when you're trying to do a feel-good proposition is to really tap into what it is that they support and things that really hit home with them. For instance," she explained, "Roxie from *106th & Park* on the BET network is from New Orleans and she goes back to help build playgrounds. You would never know that. So instead of just foisting your platform onto celebrities, find out what their passions are about and maybe your platform could fit into their specific charity."

So as you think to build your influencer-brand relationships, keep those points in mind. Here are examples of signature platforms that brands have leveraged with Bevy as influencer.

Dinners with Bevy

Dinner with Bevy is a one-of-a-kind, dining extravaganza where Smith links marketers and celebrities with movers and shakers in various fields to foster dynamic, long-lasting relationships. Smith handpicks attendees from the worlds of art, entertainment, sports, media, fashion, and philanthropy for an event that's unique, personalized, and fun. Target partnered with *Dinner with Bevy* to honor Pharrell. Amidst candlelight and friends, Target and Bevy toasted the 38-year-old super producer on his many musical accomplishments, including his gig writing the score for the 84th Annual Academy Awards. Other examples of dinners with Bevy included events at Sundance such as the Blackhouse Foundation dinner for their dedication to Black independent film and the preservation of Black cinema.

Inspired with Bevy by Range Rover

As Range Rover launched the Evoque, it partnered with Smith to create a viral talk show filmed within the car. As the urban pop culture celebrated being "fabulous," and reaching new heights, Range Rover was in the center of an inspired moment that only Bevy Smith could have created.

Smith also told me a bit about her new *Dining with Bevy: Life with Vision* platform. She's super excited about this new initiative that will provide brands with deep engagement opportunities with her core followers looking to go to the next "fabulous" level. *Dining with Bevy: Life with Vision*'s purpose is to help individuals fulfill their passions through motivational speaking and visualization exercises. Initially, Bevy created her dinner party business to connect brands with celebrities for mutually beneficial press opportunities and collaborations. *Dining with Bevy: Life With Vision* still connects people, all the while targeting young adults and helping them discover their most authentic selves. As Smith expresses it, "Think Career Day meets 'Fabulous.'"

* * *

Bloggers are the New Influencers

Bloggers are extremely influential in the world of brand marketing and have become the new celebrities. Among the most sought after are women bloggers—and Mommy Bloggers lead the way.

To build a platform that provided women bloggers with a place to express opinions and passions, three women, Lisa Stone, Elisa Camahort Page, and Jory des Jardins founded BlogHer in 2005. According to Nielsen Site Census, BlogHer attracts 40 million unique visitors per month. Visitors come to seek and share advice, opinions, and recommendations from the 3,000 blogs included in the network.

I discussed with Lisa Stone some key ways in which brands can engage bloggers, what makes a successful blogger-brand relationship and what are the relationships that work best.

Where My Girls At . . . ?

BlogHer was started to answer the question: Where are the women who blog? "In 2005," says Lisa, "this was the question coming out of the newsrooms where I worked as a journalist. At the time, I'd been blogging for a year and knew of many women who were blogging on everything from family to politics, but complaining that you're not getting attention is *not* the same thing as showing leadership. Women who blogged needed an infrastructure to do what they were doing at

the professional level. They wanted to gain additional education, grow the community of support, network on behalf of their blogs, and be paid for what they were doing."

In fact, it was a perfect storm. Why? Because at the same time marketers wanted to figure out a way to work with women who blogged.

"So," explains Lisa, "we started BlogHer as the premier media company aimed at helping bloggers and marketers achieve a business. BlogHer has become the number one cross-platform media company for women who are influential in social media and the marketers who want to work with them. We are currently in a critical transition from serving women who blog and their sponsors to serving women in social media everywhere and their sponsors. A year from now," she predicts, "BlogHer will be doing for marketers in every form of social media what we do for women who blog." My ears pricked up at the phrase "social media" and I wondered aloud what services BlogHer will be able to offer a woman in social media.

Lisa offered some astounding statistics to back up her claims. "In every study we've conducted in the past five years, BlogHer has found that there is no one more convincing to women in social media than—guess what—other women in social media. Because these women control seven trillion dollars in spending and make 85 percent of purchase decisions, it follows that businesses that want to succeed, that want to convert consumers into customers, are going to need to work more closely with her than ever before."

Lisa went on to say, "In the coming months, BlogHer is going to begin to offer the services to marketers that we currently provide in the blog space to women in the social media space." This means marketers are going to be able to work with BlogHer to reach women of influence and their followers across blogs, which still have the highest conversion rates of any marketing campaign anywhere, as well as Facebook, Twitter, Pinterest, Instagram, and whatever's coming next.

It's a huge vision as well as an amazing strategy. I asked Lisa what are the best ways they've determined to use bloggers as brand ambassadors. She explained, "Today there is no media without social media. The wonderful benefit that working with women in social media brings to brands is that, just as consumers separate signal from noise, so can marketers. Marketers know so much about who their biggest fans are including her motivations, why she buys product, and what she hopes to accomplish in her life with it. Because BlogHer knows so much about the women who visit the site at a one-to-one level, it can specialize in bringing the right women to a brand.

Stone said that "Tiffany-level" customer service is required and in a "trust" economy, time-impoverished women turn to other women because they trust them. Women also turn to organizations that serve that trust by helping them make purchases in any way they would like to do it.

Win/Win Brand-Blogger Partnership

When I brought up the subject of the right win-win brand-blogger partnership formula, Stone said that it's like any other relationship. "Both groups (brands and bloggers) have to be willing to show and say who they are, what they are doing, why they are doing it, and what they want to accomplish, and then deliver on the agreed-upon plan."

A few ways crucial points to avoid trouble are:

- It's very important for both brand and blogger to set their own expectations about what can realistically be accomplished for the budget provided. Today, 96 percent of media planners buy social media. Of that budget, according to *Chief Marketer* magazine, 17 percent are on product launches. That's the biggest chunk.

- If a brand wants a campaign that lasts longer than a 48-hour spike, it follows that a sophisticated social media strategy needs to be developed that delivers on the kind of conversation that the marketer wants to have.

- So, if a product is being brought to market with a blogger and that product does not include a media buy or does not work with a blogger who has a diversified social media following, the result will be less effective.

Stone said, "One of the things that BlogHer has learned is that Facebook is a fantastic place for keeping up with friends, for anything with regard to light entertainment, or for keeping up your public image with your friends. If the product being launched is anything remotely personal, women will not be talking about it on Facebook. Therefore, if you're working to launch a product in social media be sure to ask yourself is it the kind of product that is a good fit with all the different media out there or are there some media that are particularly powerful for it?"

Another question I discussed with Stone had to do with bloggers already in partnership with brands. How do these bloggers remain an authentic and trusted source for the network and followers as well as conveying those brand deliverables? How is the balance maintained between the authentic and trusted source and delivering on the brand message required within that partnership? Again, she made great points on this topic.

There is indeed a balance and what builds trust is disclosure. "I have learned from BlogHer's pioneering work in helping women get paid for their influence that *a brand can buy an ambassador's words but a brand cannot buy an ambassador's good opinion*. Once a brand has earned an ambassador's opinion, then it is possible for them to work together. So, the best way for a brand to succeed in social media with women is to:

- have a great product,

- find women who believe in your product, and

- make sure that these women adhere to the quality standards that BlogHer has rolled out since 2006 and which the Federal Trade Commission (FTC) has adopted.

"The FTC called us when they decided to go to market with disclosure standards and said they'd heard we were the gold standard, and what did we recommend? We believe that both visual and textual disclosure of a sponsorship helps the brand and the ambassador gain the credibility of the ambassador's good opinion. For these women in social commerce, trust is everything. The social media ambassador will never risk her community's trust by endorsing a faulty product. And the marketer needs to seek out sophisticated influencers who know better than to simply republish a press release. So, have realistic expectations and follow up these expectations with a budget.

"Then, invest that budget in a high quality endorsement campaign that reaches women where they are going in a media-appropriate way. For example, personal care does not belong on Facebook! Women don't want to talk about it there. They just want to *look* their best, not talk about how they figured out *how* to look their best. That's the difference.

Stone said, "We did a survey (conducted with Stephanie Smirnov at Devries PR, initially for P&G) called 'Beauty is in the eye of the Blogholder.' What we found is that an influential blogger is *two times more likely* to affect beauty product purchases than a national magazine beauty editor or a celebrity, and what's more, it doesn't matter if this blogger typically writes about beauty or not. She could be a food blogger, or parent blogger, or anything else."

Stone suggested an example of a great brand-blogger relationship social media campaign by Mary Kay Cosmetics. "We helped Mary Kay find bloggers who were unusually influential, and then helped them reach the right people who read these blogs. The women wrote in-depth reviews of the products that Mary Kay sent them with photographs showing their before, during, and after pictures."

She continued, "Mary Kay spent an enormous amount on the packaging of a compact with attached lipstick—it is unbelievably efficient. So, altogether it was a beauty on the go, at-home makeover kind of thing. And the packaging is very Chanel, hard black lacquer, with a beautifully subtle use of the brand. What have they done but take it super nova. They've really changed their approach. It's proof that going to those women influencing the influencers and then letting them loose to give their real opinion both visually and textually across social media is the win."

Blogging and Measurement

What about measurements to track campaigns of BlogHer with brands and bloggers? Stone agreed that could be a problem and something that brands are going to have to get used to as technology and user behavior continue to push social media. There is no universal standard but there are some measurement tools available. "In Twitter, for example, we will leverage a tool called TweetReach to measure not just the number of Tweets but also the number of unique individuals reached by these Tweets and the number of impressions delivered as part of the activity on that medium. What we're looking for are partners who are interested in working with us to innovate on that front, because we are the only organization that has seven years of data on how its campaigns performed on individual blogs. We're able to leverage that on behalf of marketers, i.e., we know who does more for chocolate and who does more for lipstick."

In looking toward the future as it relates to social media platforms, what does she think will offer a bigger opportunity for brands? Stone said the transition is from marketing *to* women to having a conversation *with* women about what they want. She added, "Because it's important not to stereotype based on gender or race, the teams that we see as the most successful in working with the primary consumers have women and people of color on their teams driving the strategy. Diverse teams," she emphasizes, "have better understanding of how to have that conversation." And indeed, brands can look to BlogHer to continue to serve as market leaders connecting with influential women in social media.

Another great way to connect with leading bloggers is for your brand to have a presence at the key blogging conferences that multicultural blogger networks pay attention to. These include Blogalicious, #Latism, Latina Mommy Bloggers, Hispanicize, Blissdom, and Blogworld. Descriptions of each of these can be found on the internet.

TAKEAWAYS

1. The process of using relationships with influential people that leads to assisting you in creating visibility for your product or service is known as influencer marketing. This type of marketing rides on the prospect of something fabulous for your potential customers, along with the audience of the influencer. It also depends on one other element—**the great relationship you build** with the influencer.

2. You've got to **recognize what your influencers care about**. How to do this? Explore their previous blog posts and articles. Peruse their clip files. See where they've been cited and interviewed.

3. If a brand wants a campaign that lasts longer than a 48-hour spike, it follows that **a sophisticated social media strategy needs to be developed** that delivers on the kind of conversation that the marketer wants to have.

4. If a product is being brought to market with a blogger and that product does not include a media buy or does not work with a blogger who has a diversified social media following, the result will be less effective. For women in social commerce, trust is everything. The social media ambassador will never risk her community's trust by endorsing a faulty product. And the marketer needs to seek out sophisticated influencers who know better than to simply republish a press release. So, **have realistic expectations and follow up these expectations with a budget**.

Chapter 11

Public Relations to Raise Awareness and Drive Engagement

Some are born great, some achieve greatness, and some hire public relations officers.
— Daniel J. Boorstin

OVER THE PAST 30 YEARS, the public relations (PR) industry has undergone dramatic changes; gone are the days when traditional media drove the conversation. Today's current PR and media landscape has evolved into a technological, socially driven machine, always-on conversation, exchanging opinions, ideas, news, content, and more. At this point, with 24/7 real-time information in a totally connected world, the PR industry itself is hard pressed to articulate its core definition.

The term "PR" itself carries a variety of different interpretations, depending on the company, the objective, and the situation. The 1982 definition of public relations, according to the Public Relations Society of America was, "Public relations helps an organization and its publics adapt mutually to each other." At the rate technology has moved in the past 20 years, such a definition has been rendered all but obsolete. Today, PR is defined in much more dynamic terms. "Public relations," according to a March 1, 2012, *New York Times* article, "is a strategic communication process that builds mutually beneficial relationships between organizations and their publics." The verbs tell the story—we've gone from adapting to building.

At the core of modern definitions lies the building of what P&G's Marc Pritchard has called "mutually beneficial and authentic relationships." Given that relationship building is at the heart of the new definition of

PR, it's expected that PR also builds emotional connections and drives engagement between brands and consumers. P&G, for example, has publicly noted that relationships are at the center of its brand-building efforts. In fact, a one-on-one relationship with each and every consumer is its goal. At the 2010 Council of PR Firms Critical Issues Forum, Pritchard noted, "I saw that PR works best when it's fully integrated into the marketing mix. I saw how PR could build emotional connections between a brand and consumer. I saw PR build relationships and convert people into becoming brand ambassadors." Pritchard also affirmed that PR was essential to purpose brand building.

When used alone, or each one independently, marketing tools produce particular results. However, when such tools are united into a 360-degree integrated marketing plan, the synergy vividly increases results.

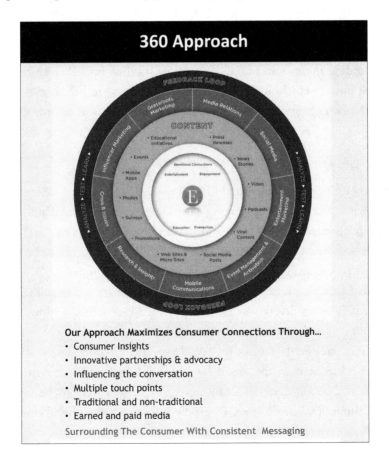

Think about it. Do you ever watch television and surf the web at the same time? According to a March 2010 ACNielsen report, you're in good company. It found that a full 60 percent of consumers both watched TV and used the internet simultaneously at least once monthly. As well, online video consumption is up 16 percent from the previous year. What does that mean? Integrated marketing efforts across various platforms have a synergistic effect. The beauty of this diverse "surround sound" can be measured in better accountability and tracking, higher retention and effectiveness in persuading consumers to buy, and more personal engagement with consumers. Looking holistically at all of the touch points surrounding the consumer, wherever they may be, includes not only a strong online component, but also television, radio, print, events, and other offline media.

To repeat, when PR is leveraged in this manner you build an emotional connection between brand and consumer and create brand evangelists to spread your message for you. At a time when people are demanding more from brands, you know it's time for PR to shine. PR is the power vehicle to bring your brand purpose to life. It can drive awareness, engagement, relationships, conversation, and advocacy.

Leveraging PR to reach multicultural audiences

Let's examine the multicultural PR and media landscape and some trends to keep in mind when leveraging PR to engage multicultural audiences with purpose platforms. Today's media landscape is always on, 24/7, and always-connected environment. Therefore, PR professionals and brands must think multi-channel and multi-property at all times.

At Egami, we take what we call a "360 Diversity Surround Sound" Approach using diverse media to drive messages across cultures. This surround sound approach is illustrated below.

Gone are the days of print, broadcast, and TV domination. Forget about a hierarchy in the media landscape. Online outlets are open for business 24/7, and social media never sleeps. You have to be prolific and "think 360," at all times, especially since the multicultural consumers' media landscape is ever-changing. How are you going to engage effectively at every level?

While traditional outlets are still important, the game plan has changed so radically with consumer's use of the internet that it's necessary to be ever-mindful of online opportunities. For multicultural audiences, certain cultural outlets are key and trusted sources. These outlets keep multicultural consumers engaged and in the loop. It's critical to know which outlets resonate and who's who within those media outlets and, of course, how they are connected. This happens through the constant building of relationships and exploration of all opportunities to partner with outlets.

To give you a multicultural media landscape cheat sheet I will share with you an "everyone you need to know" in the national multicultural media. This list is your "go to" list to consult when thinking about driving messages across cultural content (especially engaging African-American, Hispanic, and Asian-American audiences). Note, this is just a reference. Updates happen daily so to stay on top of your own *Who's Who* please go to www.egamiconsulting.com/multiculturalmedia to download the list.

Multicultural is Mainstream

Multicultural consumers have never been a more powerful force in the marketplace. With buying power exceeding $12.5 trillion, this group packs an economic wallop. While preserving heritage, cultural characteristics, behaviors, and aspirations are important, these audiences are rapidly becoming the mainstream, especially in terms of driving conversation, opinion, and trends. Therefore, you must not only communicate your multicultural initiatives and programs in multicultural media outlets, but also integrate them into your general marketing efforts and PR plans. Multicultural is the new mainstream.

Content Creation

In today's PR landscape, another top trend is content creation. Great content will set the stage for advertising that causes consumers to salivate. You need to master content marketing and raise it to even higher levels. As traditional advertising and marketing "push" campaigns fail to get results from overwhelmed or jaded consumers, it's becoming an ever more critical strategic armament.

Take a moment and think about it. How can you use content strategically in traditional, digital, and social media channels? Some of the best content marketing strategies include trends, problem solving, how to, case studies, videos, and storytelling (remember Kony?). Each has the capability to produce a big impact, when designed to show leadership, enhance reputation, and resonate with real value to important stakeholders.

We're All Publishers Now

All sorts of high-profile advocates maintain that a new Gutenberg revolution is taking place, affording brands the capability of telling their own stories. Think of sites like HSBC's Business without Borders or curation sites such as Verne Global's Green Data Center News. Content marketing strategist Joe Pulizzi foresees that the future will bring an increased concentration on brand media platforms. This includes things like P&G's Home Made Simple (homemadesimple.com), Citrix's Workshifting (workshifting.com), and American Express's Open Forum (openforum.com), i.e., "educational sites that are in line with the brand's goals and objectives."

Taking a glance at Open Forum, you'll find articles such as "5 Ways to Build Meaningful Customer Relationships," "Should Your Business be on Pinterest?", and "3 Slick Analytic Dashboards to Monitor Your Business Website." Workshifting offers articles on working from anywhere such as "5 Tips to Finding Productive Work Space," while Home Made Simple focuses on recipes, organizing, crafts, and decorating. As you ponder your purpose-inspired campaigns, what is your plan of action to devise original content and what original content can you provide for your target in order to become a trusted "go to" source?

Co-Creating Content
Ask the World

No doubt you've heard of crowd-sourcing. It's a word that gets tossed around a lot these days. Formally defined by the Macmillan Dictionary as "trying to find a way of completing a task, a solution to a problem, etc., by asking a wide range of people or organizations if they can help, typically by using the internet," it is the act of taking a job traditionally performed by a designated agent (usually an employee) and outsourcing it to an undefined, generally large group of people in the form of an open call. It is *co-creating* content with consumers who are grounded in your purpose.

The crowd-sourcing of content, solutions, and ideas will continue to grow. If your company is understaffed and unable to produce new content on its own, you can always take existing content and repurpose it accordingly, much in the same way a book publisher will check its backlist for old titles that can be re-released as e-books.

Video Grows in External and Internal Communications

Using internal YouTube-like platforms, video is a means of educating employees and helping raise talent internally. The trend is set to hasten with the growth of YouTube channels. All sorts of commercials or digital ads have had their debuts on YouTube. Hospitals are but one example of a business that makes dramatic use of this platform. The Mayo Clinic launched an internal video platform in 2011, and New York Presbyterian Hospital presents dramatic, self-narrated stories of some of its patients, including that of a child whose internal organs were removed and replaced to cure her of cancer.

As for live-streaming brief events, smartphones and flip-type cams make it easier to achieve this. In fact, television stations that once refused to run B-roll from corporations are now so short-staffed, they'll gladly air your footage of a factory floor or employee interview.

Digital Curation

Digital curation is generally described as the process of establishing and developing long term repositories of digital assets for current and future reference by researchers, scientists, historians, and scholars. Enterprises are starting to use digital curation to improve the quality of information and data within their operational and strategic processes. In the wake of content marketing, curation is an essential tactical tool. While PR is already expert at researching and gathering intelligence, what's being understood now is the budding power of packaging. This means adding value to content from various sources and presenting it. Curation's value lies in the quality of what is shared. The more significant and important the information, the more reputations are enhanced, as influence is built, and attention is gained.

Once connections are in place, PR's most important role is in building substantial communities. With social media offering such a plethora of ways to do this, the task is not to be overwhelmed! Keep it simple, as the saying goes. Pick your channels, listen to and cultivate two-way organizational communication. And never forget the importance of old-fashioned, personal communications in community building.

The Power of the Big Idea

Ultimately, creative PR is the driver of the big idea. It is also essential for your purpose initiatives and the place where the proverbial rubber meets the road. That big idea has its genesis in time spent with consumers in their homes, schools, and everyday lives, time which results in deep insights that represent truths, motivations and tensions that must be solved by the benefits of brands. From these insights come the big ideas that make them more relevant to people's lives and build the entire brand, while at the same time tying to its equity. These big ideas are so engaging, so unique, so out-of-the-box, so disruptive, they invite participation, and even movements, through word of mouth advocacy in PR, passing along YouTube videos, fans on Facebook, Twitter messages, event participation, charitable donations, and of course, purchases. Creative ideas are the essence of good PR. Lacking the queen mother of an idea, a brand's PR campaign is nothing more than a collection of old-hat PR tools; surveys, photo-calls, and celebrity endorsements, you name it. The most successful campaigns have to be fully united with a powerful creative thread joining the brand to its communications goals in a fashion that renders the most engaging and memorable effect on the target audience.

Identifying and fighting for that big idea takes courage. As noted above, it takes time, effort, and a sometimes hard-won strategic comprehension of the brand *and* its audience to unearth that "aha" that generates not only excitement, but also a host of other ideas to drive different communication channels.

Make no mistake: Creative ideas always get noticed. Sometimes they'll hit the news and become a permanent part of the linguistic lexicon. A more recent example is found in Coca-Cola's vitaminwater, when it was put directly into the hands of Facebook fans to crowdsource ideas for its next flavored drink. That's the force of a truly integrated PR campaign, powered and sustained through social media with measurable links back to brand information.

Let's look at an example of a big idea, in this case Old Spice, which changed the game.

The slogan, "Smell like a man, man" caught fire with the popular discourse, with PR waving the banner that inspired participation. Old Spice's purpose, to "help guys navigate the seas of manhood" manifested in a campaign based on the insight that men want to be masculine, while actually harboring a fear of not being manly enough. It was then  brilliantly articulated with the handsome Old Spice guy saying, "Ladies, look at your man, now look back at me, now back at your man, now back at me. Sadly, he isn't me." The solution for men is consequently simple: quit using feminine-smelling body wash and switch to Old Spice.

The first commercial received a whopping 20 million views on YouTube. This was followed up by a Twitter campaign where the Old Spice guy answered questions—the PR team helped choose the right people to respond to based on Twitter followings. For example, Alyssa Milano had more than one million followers. Nearly 200 videos were filmed over just a few days to respond to key influencers like Ellen DeGeneres, Milano, and even everyman Johannes Beals—a regular guy asking the Old Spice guy's help in proposing to his girlfriend.

The Old Spice Guy became an instant celebrity who frequented the talk show circuit. Engagement continued to go through the roof to a 2700 percent increase in Twitter followers, 800 percent increase in Facebook interaction, a 300 percent increase to the brand website, and 140 million YouTube views (including some fan-generated spoofs). Yes, and in just a few short weeks this creative, original campaign produced over two billion PR impressions, too. This is but one spectacular example of the power of PR, especially social media-impacted PR, to amplify big ideas and generate across-the-board participation.

Another good big idea touts yet another old-time, well-known product, blasting it out of the past with a whole new reason for being. The big idea for Head & Shoulders shampoo was that the secret to football star's Troy Palomalu's incredibly full and thick hair is Head & Shoulders Hair Endurance for Men, and it was PR that started the conversation about the brand.

What happened? Head & Shoulders announced it was taking out a $1 million insurance policy on Troy's trademark hair. The story was seeded with influential online media and it took off like a rocket. In less than a week, more than one thousand stories were generated in media outlets worldwide, accompanied by thousands of Tweets, online conversations and blog comments. More than 600 million online and offline media impressions were generated in a matter of days, with television programs like *Jimmy Kimmel Live* keeping the conversation going.

Although not tied to a cause, these examples are platforms linked to brand purpose that were fun/exciting in nature and succeeded in driving word of mouth.

Pitching in Today's Environment

As you pitch your purpose initiatives, there are a number of factors to be aware of. First, print editors in their 20s and 30s have a good grasp of digital and social media. A major trend among newspapers and online-only outlets, in this DSM age, is the shift to local content. For magazines, 2011 was similar to 2010 in that the industry saw more titles launch than fold. The reason? Look to (cue the Hallelujah chorus) the iPad. Rather than killing print media (as was feared), it is having just the opposite effect, especially when people can carry their *New York Times*, their *Wall Street Journal*, their *Vogue* and *Vanity Fair* plus a lot more, all in one small device.

How about TV? Well, stations are sharing resources and using their websites to fill the gap left by shrinking newspapers. And radio, dubbed by one wag, "the great survivor," now has, according to Arbitron (the medium's primary measurement tool), more than 240 million listeners age 12 and over per week. Bloggers are partnering with a lot of mainstream media outlets and growth in the blogosphere is primarily in the consumer sector. This includes blogs about domesticity, parenting and cooking.

All of these transformations mean at least seven things for the PR industry:

1. *Make it easy for reporters.* Journalists, like everyone, are hard pressed for time and the easier you can make it for a reporter to write a story, the better your chances of clinching the deal. It also heralds that all-important good relationship between you and the writer.

2. *Buy an iPhone and/or iPad.* With the media creating content for these platforms, you need to be personally familiar with them.

3. *Don't pitch via social media.* Eighty percent of journalists prefer to be contacted through email.

4. *Media outlets want more than just text.* They're looking for pictures and video, too.

5. *Get to know journalists on social media platforms.* Follow their Tweets. But unless you know them personally, don't "friend" them on Facebook.

6. *Pitch the TV newsroom between eight and nine in the morning, if possible.* Then it precedes the daily staff meeting. Also, unless it's breaking news, pitch your story at least a few days or a week in advance. Bear in mind, too, that television journalists want to speak with real people affected by your product, not just your CEO or spokesperson.

7. *The old rules for pitching still apply.* Last but not least, just because social media has rocked the boat doesn't mean it's a different boat. It's the same one and while it's true old-media companies are evolving, this doesn't mean they merit different treatment. Hold fast to the traditional etiquette of introduction first and questions later.

Peaking Your Pinterest: Pinterest for PR

- **Storytelling.** Pinterest is an ideal platform for storytelling. And when it comes to PR, storytelling trumps direct promotions. A picture, as the saying goes, is worth a thousand words and a series of pictures can create millions of stories. Pinterest is all about pictures.

- **Visual Experience.** Encourage your customers to share interesting items, thereby encouraging participation and improving the overall appeal of your board.

- **Videos.** Videos represent the less publicized aspect of Pinterest. As a PR tool, a company can use Pinterest videos to educate users about its history or to address any issues by pinning them to the board.

- **Contests.** Pinterest is a great platform for contests to spread the word on your business's products and services. Originate some innovative contest ideas, ask customers to re-pin, participate on specific boards, or create boards on their own. Everyone loves contests, don't they?

- **Events.** If you attend any trade shows or conferences, share the pictures and videos on your Pinterest board. Many users routinely use Pinterest to gather more information about such events.

- **Contribute.** Pinterest is a platform where you can contribute to other boards and earn recognition. If you contribute, like, and share other Pinterest users' boards and items with similar interests, you've got yourself a passive PR tool for your business.

- **Balance.** It's important to find the right balance on Pinterest for your social media efforts. You don't do enough and your efforts will go unrecognized. You overdo it and bingo!—too much of a good thing.

PR is one of the disciplines that can unleash the power of purpose-inspired campaigns. It also plays an important role in the operations of businesses and organizations of all sizes, shapes, and colors. And, courtesy of the internet, its value as a versatile tool in getting your company's name out there has increased a hundredfold. This means turning Facebook, Pinterest, Twitter and other online properties into magnets for your audience.

TAKEAWAYS

1. Today's current PR and media landscape have evolved into a **technological, socially driven machine, always-on conversation, exchanging opinions, ideas, news, content, and more. Gone are the days of print, broadcast, and TV domination**. Forget about a hierarchy in the media landscape. Online outlets are open for business 24/7 and social media never sleeps. You have to be prolific and "think 360," at all times, especially since the multicultural consumers' media landscape is ever-changing.

2. Integrated marketing efforts across various platforms have a synergistic effect. The beauty of **this diverse "surround sound" can be measured** in better accountability and tracking, higher retention and effectiveness in persuading consumers to buy, and more personal engagement with consumers.

3. Multicultural consumers have never been a more powerful force in the marketplace. With buying power exceeding $12.5 trillion, this group packs an economic wallop. While preserving heritage, cultural characteristics, behaviors, and aspirations are important, **these audiences are rapidly becoming the mainstream**, especially in terms of driving conversation, opinion, and trends. So remember, don't limit your multicultural PR efforts to multicultural media outlets only, include the mainstream outlets as well.

Chapter 12

Purpose vs. Profit

Profit is not the legitimate purpose of business. The legitimate purpose of business is to provide a product or service that people need and do it so well that it's profitable.

—James Rouse

LEADING WITH PURPOSE is an honorable objective and one that resonates throughout this book. But lest we forget: Purpose *without profit* comes up empty. Always keep profitability in mind.

The Value of Relationship

As you examine the profitability of a business, the real currency is your ability to make connections and build relationships. Whether a B2B or B2C, the majority of your efforts are centered around your customer relationships. Which would you prefer—a shot-in-the-dark blind date, or a great night out with an old and trusted friend? The latter? Me, too. The first choice could go in any direction, with no future promises, while the second represents a familiar history with dependable prospects. And just as long-term commitments are the name of the game in personal relationships, so the same holds true in marketing. In order to better serve consumers, brands must first build a genuine, honest relationship with them. But is there a direct marketing route to consumers' subconscious minds? Yes, through purpose.

According to Jim Stengel, former P&G global marketing officer and now CEO of his own company, purpose is not only important, it is the *expectation* of today's consumer. This is amply illustrated in the "Stengel 50," a ten-year growth study of 50,000 brands. (That's right: *50,000.*) As described in Stengel's best-seller, *Grow*, the study proves how the world's fifty best businesses (ranging from companies as varied as Red Bull, Zappos, Innocent, Samsung, Method, Lindt, Discovery Communications, and Visa) enjoy a cause/effect relationship between fiscal results, and relating to people's basic hopes, dreams, and values.

This "framework," as Stengel says, has as its core principle ". . . the importance of having a *brand ideal,* a shared goal of improving people's lives. A brand ideal," he continues, "is a business's essential reason for being, the higher-order benefit it brings to the world. A brand ideal of improving people's lives is the only sustainable way to recruit, unite, and inspire all the people a business touches from its employees to its customers." Miss that connection, and the plain truth is that your brand risks the possibility of not having longevity. Another plain truth? Business growth accelerates with an inspiring ideal at the company's center.

As we've seen, the move toward ideals or purpose-driven organizations is gaining momentum on many fronts. You can see it from aging baby boomers to angel investors backing start-ups with social impact, to second careers in areas that matter to improving people's lives. I also see this with the emerging generation of young professionals who bring to the workplace a vital commitment to the importance of purpose and balance. Both of these cohorts are going to be important enablers of the "ideals powered brands" that Stengel is espousing.

Allow me to let you in on the "400 Percent Advantage" model. This 400 Percent Advantage demystifies corporate growth in an exciting and fascinating way. During the early part of the new century, the Stengel 50—those brands involved in Stengel's ten-year growth study mentioned previously—produced a return on investment at an astonishing 400 percent above the Standard & Poor's 500. How do they do it? Well, for one thing the Stengel 50 are "operating in harmony with their brand ideals." Most importantly, Stengel emphasizes the fact that this is not to be confused with some kind of corporate social responsibility or philanthropy:

It's about expressing a business's fundamental reason for being and powering its growth. It's about linking and leveraging the behaviors of all the people important to a business's future, because nothing unites and motivates people's actions as strongly as ideals. They make it possible to connect what happens inside a business with what happens outside it, especially in the "black box" of people's minds and how they make decisions. Ideals are the ultimate driver, my research has found, of category-leading growth.

When "nothing motivates people's actions as strongly as ideals," the sky is the limit for growth, as the Stengel 50 and the 400 Percent Advantage have proven beyond the shadow of a doubt.

Simple questions, such as how well we understand the people most important to our future, or what does our brand stand for or want to stand for, and how we're addressing these issues, fuel the fire toward answers—answers that Stengel identifies as "five activities [that] constitute an extraordinarily powerful business growth system." These answers are also key ROI drivers. Here is how Stengel describes these activities:

Discovering, or rediscovering, a brand ideal in one of five fields of fundamental human values [see below].

Building the business culture around the ideal.

Communicating the ideal internally and externally to engage employees and customers.

Delivering a near-ideal customer experience.

Evaluating business progress and people against the ideal.

Then, take the beliefs of the people who work for the business (think of the brand's heritage here), and the inherent shared values between customers and end users and what have you got? A winning recipe for success.

Think of a social media company mentioned frequently throughout these pages, the ubiquitous Facebook. With 100 percent of its business model concentrated on connecting its users, Facebook has created inexorable value worldwide. And while Facebook, a pure product of the digital age, may not have a heritage to evoke, let's look at two other products that do have just that.

The first is the renowned French luxury line of Louis Vuitton. Founded in the 19th century by a young apprentice baggage maker of the same name, the line has a 200-year history of being synonymous with high-end luggage and handbags. More than that, it is an $8 billion brand with gorgeous stores throughout the world. But is that all? Not by a long shot. A brand that already celebrated travel, it launched a "Core Values" campaign to animate the company's ideal. You've probably seen the glossy magazine ads with global humanitarian figures such as Bono, Mikhail Gorbachev, and Angelina Jolie on life-changing journeys, carrying the inimitable LV gear. The message could not be stronger, especially with Jolie photographed in Cambodia where she has both represented the United Nations and adopted a child.

The other brand is Dove, a product you've known since childhood for providing smooth, non-drying cleanliness. But Dove has also become known for its brand ideal to "celebrate every woman's unique beauty," which transcends individual attractiveness to bring about a sea change in the way beauty itself is apprehended in society. Thanks to this evolution in thinking, all people can feel better about who they are and how they look.

These two products, at opposite ends of the marketing food chain, reflect what Jim Stengel calls "Five Fields of Fundamental Human Values." They are:

- Eliciting Joy
- Enabling Connection
- Inspiring Exploration
- Evoking Pride
- Impacting Society

Think about it: how is your brand serving its audience in at least one of these five categories? If it's not in the running for any of them, then it is probably not in the running for significant growth, either.

Now that we know that purpose-led companies are truly profitable, let's think about some ROI drivers to keep top of mind.

Long-Term Commitment versus One-off Support

- Brands that want to serve people and their communities must have long-term commitments when bringing their brand purpose to life. When you come to a multicultural community, your plan had better be long-term and not just a one-hit sensation.

- African Americans and Hispanics tend to be skeptical about brands being short-term, "in and out" types of businesses.

- A high percent of multicultural consumers have low expectations of new businesses in their communities.

A Winning Example: Long-term Commitment

As I began work on this chapter, I received an email from multicultural marketer, Belinda M. Wilson. As the associate manager of Domestic Multicultural Marketing at Disney Destinations, Belinda's core program there is Disney's Dreamers Academy, where she oversees its marketing strategy and development. Now entering its sixth year, the program has become a staple of the African-American community, not to mention a favorite purpose-inspired initiative of my own.

In its first year, 2008, Disney's Dreamers Academy had a purpose grounded in making dreams come true for young multicultural students throughout United States. Disney, a historic company founded on Walt's immortal words, "If you can dream it, you can do it," formed

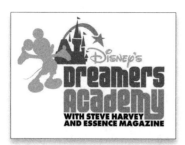

a dedicated mission to the future of young people, teaching selected youths to harness the power of their dreams. From there, these young dreamers learn not just to motivate themselves, but also to inspire their friends, families and communities.

"DDA" has evolved from a promotional initiative to a key pillar in the strategic initiative for the African-American segment of Disney's audience. It begins with a call-out to students aged 13 to 18—the critical make-or-break years in a young person's life. Out of some 5,000 applications, 100 are chosen. These 100 youngsters are not just your typical over-achievers, either. Each application essay is carefully scrutinized and evaluated for key characteristics of:

- intellectual curiosity,

- leadership qualities,

- courage,

- compassion.

The winners then attend a four-day event at Disney World, where they engage in a specially designed, challenging and fun curriculum led by Disney cast members. The message is instilled that it takes a village, and a village of support is just what they have behind them as they explore personal goals and possible career paths, such as culinary, engineering, and executive Disney World, which is amply suited to provide the perfect showcase for multiple professional fields. This career "deep dive" leverages Disney's internal resources for further career support to youngsters.

The three elements that govern the event are:

1. Dreaming big

2. Discovering a world of possibilities

3. Preparing to achieve dreams

Students come away with tangible tools to implement in their lives and share with others in their home communities. This ensures that focus is retained. And, while a general "community relations" feel may seem to prevail, the program is specifically structured to create a strong emotional connection with African-American consumers who can see firsthand Disney's commitment to the their community via DDA. More importantly, DDA ties to Disney's brand purpose, providing creative, innovative experiences that inspire and teach. DDA aligns with that brand purpose and takes it a step further, in demonstrating to African-American consumers their commitment to them while at the same time, linking Black consumers' commitment to brand loyalty and affinity.

Since Wilson has come on board with DDA, it has become much more than just an event. According to her, with five students selected from 500 alumnae to be brand advocates and spokespersons, the word is further spread nationwide about Disney's active commitment to multicultural youth. Needless to say, the active engagement of Disney employees in the program further deepens its impact throughout the entire company.

From a marketing standpoint, Wilson emphasizes, "It's another way to show our commitment to the community. We also have other programs at Disney that target youth such as the Youth Education Series (YES) initiative; however, the value of the internal partnership is clear when you think of what we are able to offer to thousands of students through our YES Program here at Disney World—that is how we evolved our career 'Deep Dives' and just throwing that out exponentially has also kept the elements in play far above and beyond the four day event."

When I asked Wilson about the power of aligning influencers and celebrities to do good works, I also touched on the history of Steve Harvey's partnership with DDA. She responded that among the things they looked for when first starting the program was:

- someone who had a very pronounced, trusted voice in the African-American community, and was connected to them;

- an individual who shared similar passions and objectives as DDA, and who was really focused on developing and inspiring African-American youth.

These components led Disney to Steve Harvey. "He has a heart for young men and understands that there's a void and a need in the Black community to continue that character development. Then, we shared our perspective, i.e., that we did not want to focus exclusively on boys.

There was a bigger opportunity here, across the board. So, we came together with Steve through ideation and collaboration. We already had DDA in place and realized what a trusted and credible voice Harvey has in the African-American community. We asked him his views on DDA, especially since Disney (at that time) did not really have a foothold there." Steve Harvey helped them think it through and his own passion made it clear that he was the right person to go with. With 8.5 million listeners to his radio show (this was before his books came out) and 96 percent of that audience being African American, it's easy to see why Harvey aligned so well with Disney's target for DDA.

"I can't say enough about Steve Harvey's genuine commitment to our youth. His enthusiasm and passion, insofar as taking the DDA kids under his wing," says Wilson, "especially in terms of his one-on-one relationships with them (keeping it friendly and magical for Disney!). He is a father himself who understands the needs of teenagers and is invested in seeing them grow beyond society's expectations."

It's interesting to see how Harvey has evolved his personal brand from starting out in comedy, to television, to an anchor with radio. He's also a big Disney fan who believes in the company and has already done several Vacation Club experiences. As Wilson stresses, he's already been a part of the portfolio overall, who understands their brand and the particular segment of African-American consumers that they were targeting. Harvey has emphasized the necessity, in terms of his DDA partnership, of his giving back to the community and that DDA was something he *had* to do, as a Black man with children. He also has an innate understanding of kids who've survived difficult times, and wants them to be in an environment where they can see other individuals who have achieved success and show those kids that they, too, can make it. As Wilson says, "he resonates as a credible icon within the Black community," and is compelled to give back.

DDA has more recently partnered with Essence. "As *Essence* is a place where African-American women go to consult on everything from beauty to family, partnering with them made great sense, too," Wilson explained. "They also have a huge commitment to youth because if parents are empowered that translates down to generations to come. So, *Essence* is a critical partner with Disney, a communications partner who helps us to extend the DDA message, one that resonates more with the overall target that we're trying to reach with Black consumers."

How, I wondered, do you measure the success of the DDA? Wilson pointed to two primary ways in which executives at Disney see DDA.

Tracking

The program was created so that Disney had a more relevant connection with the Black consumer, and what it learned is that African-American consumers want to experience the Disney theme parks just the much as anyone else does. Disney tracks students to view their continued success—simple metrics like how many students finish high school and move forward with college. When students write back to Disney and share updates regarding career choices that occurred as a result of DDA, that is how they gauge success for each student. Obviously, Disney does not discredit the students' own support systems of family, school, and church. But they do measure specific decisions students make as a result of DDA, along with academic matriculation rates. Also, they measure the amount of volunteering that the students do—for example, one young lady was accepted to serve on President Clinton's Youth Committee for Overcoming Childhood Obesity.

Surveys

In order to find consumer insights, they survey theme park guests for their awareness level of DDA and how it affects their perception of Disney. This is a way to directly link success of the program to customer perception, although it is careful *not* to link the increased number of African American visitors to Disney theme parks with DDA. However, it is seen as an indirect result.

Wilson will say that the Disney visitors who are aware of DDA definitely feel more comfortable spending their dollars there, and that Disney's success with African-American consumers would not be the same without DDA. "Across multiple disciplines," she explains, "it's interesting that word of mouth will always be a huge factor for our success, because when a parent or guardian or volunteer experiences the magic of Disney, the word spreads. Both qualitative and quantitative research shows that DDA feedback (on social media, too) accounts for a lot of new visitors."

Wilson points out, "We think about how our brand is relevant to this consumer, activations are designed from that perspective. But it has to be specific—for example, bringing Princess Tiana to New Orleans, her home. This makes Disney unique and the purpose of events is to whet appetites for more of the Disney experience."

Finally, I talked with Wilson about the future. What should brands do less or more of for multicultural audiences? This time, her answer was threefold:

The first thing is to understand all facets of your consumer—who they are and what their world is like—and the nuances of what they believe about your brand. What role does your brand play in their lives? Refine your target *from* there.

The second thing is to keep your hand on the pulse of what the consumer is constantly thinking about you. Develop your strategies to have room for adjustment. Maintaining a dialogue and keeping channels open is key to keeping your consumer engaged. Let them feel spoken to rather than marketed at. P&G nailed this with *My Black is Beautiful* (see Chapter Two).

The third is to understand where the gaps are. You must be able to identify the right purpose-driven initiatives with which to align your brand, and they've got to be core to who your brand is. DDA was born out of this. Be relevant to your consumer at all times!

• • •

Mindshare versus Wallet share

For those marketers looking to measure effective ROI, another helpful tip is to aim for mindshare versus wallet share.

According to Fernando Molinar, associate director of multicultural marketing for Verizon Wireless, Northeast (VZE NE), "you can't do the same thing all the time." You need to get into the shoes, into the psyche, of that Hispanic, African-American, or Asian-American customer, and understand what drives their purchasing. "Without a mindshare," he states, "you won't get a wallet share. You have to drive that consumer to believe in your brand, to trust your brand and *want* to be loyal to it, and guess what: you're not going to achieve that by focusing on sales strategy alone."

Let's take a look at how VZW NE prioritizes the Asian-American "mindshare." But first, just who *is* the Asian-American consumer? In *Multicultural Intelligence: Eight Make or Break Rules for Marketing to Race, Ethnicity and Sexual Orientation* (Paramount Market Publishing, Inc., 2009), David R. Morse offers the following helpful facts:

- There were 15 million Asian Americans in 2007. In 1970, there were fewer than a million. Between 2000 and 2005, this population grew by 19.8 percent (the Hispanic population grew by 20.9 percent). Nearly half of all Asians live in either California or New York.

- Chinese make up the largest subgroup of Asians (the Census tracks 10); they make up about 23 percent of the Asian population (excluding Taiwanese), followed by Asian Indians and Filipinos who make up 19 percent and 18 percent, respectively. The two fastest growing subgroups are Pakistanis and Asian Indians, which grew by 36 percent and 34 percent respectively between 2000 and 2005.

- As a group, Asian Americans are educated and affluent. Nearly half have a bachelor's degree or more and they are the most likely group to work in managerial or professional jobs (46 percent compared with 36 percent of non-Hispanic Whites). The median income of Asian-American households is 26 percent higher than the U.S. average. Still, there are disparities between different ethnic groups. For instance, the median annual household income for Asian Indians and Filipinos is $69,000 and $66,000, respectively. For Cambodians, it's $36,000 and for Hmong it's $32,000.

- Asian Americans are primarily an immigrant population, with slightly over two-thirds being foreign born. As is the case with income, there are differences by ethnicity. About three-quarters of Koreans and Asian Indians are foreign born compared with about two-thirds of Chinese and Filipinos. Nearly six in ten Japanese Americans were born in the United States. Also, there are big differences by age. While 80 percent of Asian adults are immigrants, about 80 percent of Asians under the age of 19 were born in the United States.

These statistics clearly show that Asian Americans are educated and affluent, so designing a particular initiative for them had to call those elements into play. Molinar gives the example of one program, wherein Verizon Wireless came up with out-of-the-box ways to leverage insight and deliver on an unmet need to the segment. The result was "Asian Pacific American Visionaries: Innovate. Inspire. Rule." How did it work? Well, as in life, timing played a major role. In honor of May's Asian Pacific American Heritage Month, consumers were invited to register for an evening conference in the Grand Ballroom at the East Village's historic Webster Hall. Hosted by Filipina-American internet personality Christina Gambito (aka Happyslip), the panel of speakers included such iconic Asian Americans as Hollywood film producer Teddy Zee, supermodel Jenny Shimizu, martial artist Cung Le, and MTV news correspondent SuChin Pak.

There was also an exciting contest for future visionaries who submitted videos describing:

- *What is your idea and what makes it visionary?*

- *How can a $5,000 grant aid in helping your idea become a reality?*

- *How would you envision integrating Verizon Wireless's wireless technology in the practical application of your idea?*

The top three video submissions with the most "Likes" on Facebook were invited to attend the conference, where the winner was announced and became eligible to win the $5,000 grand prize and other great prizes. You can see from the scope of both the conference and contest that Verizon understood its Asian American audience as particularly tech savvy, entrepreneurially driven, and very into establishing their own individual innovation. "How great was it," Molinar asks, "to marry that brand segment with Verizon's brand goal?" It was accomplished by recognizing, inciting, and rewarding people who came up with new ideas, and a prize that came with a lot of eyes on it.

The advice Molinar offers to marketers who want to get into this space and be aggressive, who are looking to attract the multicultural audience, is, number one: commitment. Multicultural consumers are quick to spot a lightweight who's here one minute and gone the next. So if you're having thoughts along the lines that, "oh, it's Asian-American Heritage month, let's get it done with and leave," forget it. Not just you as leader, but your entire staff has to live and breathe its total commitment.

His second bit of advice? "You've got to keep up with trends. You've got to know what—whether it's Black, Hispanic or Asian—what are they doing? Where is their playground? What are they buying or not buying, what are their barriers to buying? What really motivates them? The answer is *not* just to throw a Black/Hispanic/Asian person in your print ad. It doesn't even resonate." When representing a particular ethnic person be absolutely specific and choose, for example, a Black graduate of an HBCU rather than a generic photograph with no explicit connection to anything.

• • •

Commitment to the Cause

I had a chance to speak with P&G assistant brand manager Martin Anka-mah, who served as Bounty multicultural manager and who executed, along with his team, many of the programs discussed earlier such as *Bounty Teacher's Wish List, Make a Clean Difference, Make a Messterpiece* and more. Ankamah has played a significant role in overseeing the multicultural strategy and execution for the brand. Here is what he had to say about long-term commitments as a key ROI driver. According to his expertise, each year you're going to get more efficient and more ROI for the investment that you do because people see your brand's commitment to its cause and it's not just "here today, gone tomorrow." That's always a risk. "Some people in some communities may think, oh, this is just some corporate thing and not substantial. So, you need to go into it saying this is really about serving and yes, we do need to turn an ROI. And let's invest in a way that by year two or year three that we see ourselves at a place where our investment is declining in terms of the actual spent production dollars, *but* we're able to see more media pick-up, more traction, more excitement—we're tweaking the idea, we're improving and then from there we should get better. So, that would be my advice. I think it's possible to come out with a big hit in year one, but I don't think if you don't that you're an anomaly or that you should give up. You need to be committed to the cause and as you set a goal be strategic in how you achieve that goal to improve year on year. And also make sure you work with partners who you believe can help you be trustful, who can help you amplify your reach and that can help maybe save some of your dollars."

TAKEAWAYS

1. As you examine the profitability of a business, the real currency is your ability to **make connections and build relationships.** Whether a B2B or B2C, the majority of your efforts are centered around your customer relationships.

2. "A brand ideal," according to Jim Stengel, former P&G global marketing officer

and now CEO of his own company, "is a business's essential reason for being, the higher-order benefit it brings to the world. A **brand ideal of improving people's lives** is the only sustainable way to recruit, unite, and inspire all the people a business touches from its employees to its customers." Miss that connection, and the plain truth is that your brand risks the possibility of not having longevity. Another plain truth? Business growth accelerates with an inspiring ideal at the company's center.

3. Brands that want to serve people and their communities must have long-term commitments when bringing their brand purpose to life. When you come to a multicultural community, **your plan had better be long-term** and not just a one-hit sensation.

4. For those marketers looking to measure effective ROI, another helpful tip is to aim for **mindshare** versus wallet share.

Chapter 13

Align Your Purpose With Your Career

Everyone has a purpose in life—a unique gift or special talent to give others, and for every unique talent and expression of that talent, there are also unique needs. When we blend this unique talent with service to others, we experience the ecstasy and exultation of spirit. This is the goal of all goals.

—Deepak Chopra

YOU KNOW THE SAYING, "Save the best for last." Well, in this case the best is you. In these final chapters, I'd like to challenge you to ponder what does purpose mean to you? What is your personal purpose? How is it connected to your professional life? Are you living a purpose-inspired life every day? What's your role in the future of purpose-inspired marketing? The most important element behind purpose-inspired solutions are purpose-inspired people.

Whether a brand manager, a CEO, a student, or an entrepreneur, each of us must feel that our lives have meaning in our day-to-day duties. Ask yourself: is your career aligned to your calling? It takes the right person for the right job. In his book, *Good to Great: Why Some Companies Make the Leap . . . and Others Don't* (Collins, 2001), Jim Collins puts it this way:

> *First who, then what.* We expected that good-to-great leaders would begin by setting a new vision and strategy. We found instead that they *first* got the right people on the bus, the wrong *people* off the

bus, and the right people in the right seats—and *then* they figured out where to drive it. The old adage "people are your best asset" turns out to be wrong. People are *not* your most important asset. The *right* people are."

Think of the "right seat" as being your purpose. Here are my personal beliefs about purpose. First, I believe that your purpose is connected to something greater than yourself—your passions are tied directly to your God-given gifts. Great ideas and new innovations are born in the spiritual realm and *those* are the ones that are connected to something greater than yourself; in fact, they have a destiny of their own and they are the ones that you will be great at. It is my belief that purpose-inspired businesses that stand for something greater than themselves are the ultimate goal.

Discover Your Purpose

As you ponder purpose; I think Jim Collins' *Good to Great* offers key questions worth examining:

What are you deeply passionate about?

What can you be the best in the world at?

What drives your economic engine?

Those questions are summed up by the Hedgehog Concept. Here it is in a nutshell. Beginning with the fable comparing the speedy fox to the slow, methodical hedgehog, Collins illustrates that hedgehogs, while not exciting, are always consistent. He compares Good-to-Great companies to that little hedgehog who is always focused on his consistent method of success. Out of this little tale, Collins developed his Hedgehog Concept.

The Hedgehog Concept is neither a goal, nor strategy or plan to be the best. Rather—and this distinction is critical—it is an *understanding* of what you can be best at, and defining that.

What generates robust cash flow and profitability? The Good-to-Great companies recognize the single denominator (profit per x) that has the strongest impact on their economics. The key is to use the question of the denominator to gain insight into your economic model.

What are you most passionate about? The good-to-great companies focus only on those activities that motivate their passions. This is not something that can be manufactured; it can only be discovered, person by person.

These three core concepts combined with the fanatical consistency of the Hedgehog Concept drove the Good-to-Great companies to consistently create great results. Of course, finding your own Hedgehog Concept isn't easy. As you can guess by the name, it takes time. Therefore, author Collins suggests implementing a team of counselors to oversee the process. So, put this book down for a moment and think about it: What are you best in the world at? What drives your economic engine? What are you passionate about?

Stay Spiritually Connected to a Source Greater than Yourself

There were two influential books that I read at the start of my purpose-inspired journey that helped me to connect my personal purpose and profession, and also connect my career and calling, and my understanding that it was connected to a divine plan.

As discussed in prior chapters, early on in the course of my purpose-inspired journey, I was named by Russell Simmons to serve as General Manager of RUSH Communications. This appointment came exactly one year to the day from the time that I started volunteering with Simmons. I was 27 and wondered how in the world I would gain respect and make a difference in this company. Though super excited, I also realized that with this position came a great deal of responsibility. So, in search of knowledge and material that would help shape my personal leadership style, I started to research books on the subject.

Eventually, I came across *God Is My CEO: Following God's Principles in a Bottom-Line World* by Larry Julian (Adams Media, 2002). A business development and leadership coach providing counsel to a range of Fortune 100/500 corporate leaders, Julian was able to support leaders in understanding how to marry their spiritual beliefs and business acumen together to serve a greater good. Acutely sensitive to the internal battles occurring in the midst of many leaders, he offered a unique perspective on what it means to be purpose-led in a bottom-line world. At the root of Julian's teachings, he embraces servant-style leadership. The heart of purpose principals is ensuring that we are connected to how our gifts, our offerings, and products serve others and the world at large. The book's title resonated deeply with my spirit at a time when I was developing my personal leadership style; I knew I wanted to be connected to something greater.

Business Principles versus God's Principles

UNWRITTEN BUSINESS RULES **Achieve results**	GOD'S PRINCIPLES **Serve a purpose**
• What can I get?	• How can I give?
• Success = dollars	• Significance = people
• Work to please people	• Work to please God
• Fear of the unknown	• Living with hope
• Take charge; surrender means defeat	• Leadership is being last
• The end justifies the means. Get to the outcome regardless of how you accomplish it	• Let go; surrender means victory
• Short-term gain	• The means justify the end. Do the right thing regardless of the outcome
• Slave to urgent	• Long-term legacy
• You can never produce enough	• Freedom of choice
	• Unconditional love

From God is My CEO

Great Mind #1. Let's start with Larry Julian

Julian has found the balance in supporting leaders to avoid the mistake of treating their spirituality as something completely separate from their business. As you can see in the chart above, questions like "what can I get" are poised against "what can I give," "short term gain" versus "long term legacy" and so forth. Julian's influence on me was profound and I was delighted when he accepted my invitation to be interviewed for this book and talk about leading with purpose.

Let Who You Are Speak for What you Believe

According to Julian, "a workplace can be opposite to faith values. That is a continuing challenge. Let who you are speak for what you believe. Show respect and support, love people, be a generous individual who helps them with their time. There are 1,001 ways in which your behavior, your actions, your decisions, and your life have an impact on people around you. So that's the simplest thing you could do but the implications of it are huge. And just by being who you are, people can be attracted to you and what you have to say. You can have a great impact. Let who you are speak for what you believe."

Be Centered Enough to Listen to Your Spirit for Guidance

"Be led by spirit versus emotion. You could be at peace in the moment and ready for the day and within four minutes something happens to set you off! Tons of problems and challenges assail us daily. Leaders are in REACT mode, with emotions like anger, fear, and knee-jerk reaction to solve problems, bypassing the core issue. Being led by spirit means being centered enough to listen to the spirit in terms of your response. If you're worried and fearful about problems from work to home, worried about losing an account or even your job, 'as a man thinketh, he becomes.' The actions you take as a result of such emotions can potentially lead you down the wrong path. But if you follow your spirit, don't judge others, are forgiving, patient and kind, you'll be led by the spirit and in partnership with God. That has positive consequences."

Purpose is a Long-Term Business Growth Strategy

When I had the chance to ask him about the advice he would give companies about leading with purpose, he began, "Obviously part of your role as a CEO is to deliver profits. The challenge is when profits are the driver over your sense of purpose, then things go awry. It's a matter of understanding how they're married together. As an example, if you are just led by profit, you are becoming a slave to the bottom line. Your actions, decisions, orders are only about achieving that end. It's very short term, whereas purpose is an *eternal* perspective, a long-term perspective. If you have an organization that serves a greater purpose it outlives the short-term challenges that you face. That's why purpose is a priority over profits. Take it from the standpoint of employees. If you ask employees what motivates them, you can say money—a paycheck is clearly a motivator. But that motivation will only last for so long. Again, the goal is that you have a financial responsibility to earn a profit but serving a purpose will get you the profits if you're doing it right and with excellence."

Let Your Mission Be Your Purpose Guide

Having heard that there are tactical things a leader can do, I asked Julian if he had any particular steps to offer. "Yes," he answered immediately. "Two important steps. Step number one is that you have an obligation to God and others to remain spiritually healthy. What I mean by that is that there is always going to be a battle or a tension between ego and God, or control and surrender, or pride and humility. Everything starts from the top down and the leader needs to maintain humility and integrity in himself, that's number one, and hopefully he has trusted peers who are holding him accountable. Number two is that, as you go to the senior leadership you need a solid leadership team who are always challenging themselves to maintain the mission and the values of the organization. After that, obviously you're instilling those values throughout the organization and there are many methods to do that. But always let your mission be the true leader and guide."

The Ultimate Marriage of your Career and Calling Leads to Purpose Matrimony

"Young people face myriad challenges when they enter into business, whether in an organization or as an entrepreneur." Yes, I agreed. But how can young adults, leaders, entrepreneurs and employees integrate their career with their calling? "If your perspective or priorities are not right," Julian replied, "you are prone to a) lose focus or b) let that career take over your life, getting swept away, without it being aligned with your calling. What has God called you to be and do? Os Guinness, author of *The Call: Finding and Fulfilling the Central Purpose of Your Life* (Thomas Nelson, 1998), basically says you can quit a job but you can't quit your calling. It's true. God has called you for a reason and a purpose, he's called you to Him. My job changes but I'm always centered in asking God where he wants me to be. Part of this process for young entrepreneurs is understanding a sense of what your calling is, looking at things from an eternal perspective—what is it that matters here, what are you doing and how are you part of God's larger story and plan? Where do you make a difference? And then the ideal thing is to marry the two."

Find Great Meaning in Your Day-to-Day Work. Find a Higher Calling in it.

"Whether you're working in a company or as an entrepreneur, there are days that are drudgery. Or even just working at a company where you're not valued. So what's important in that regard is that *God* has called us. Work is worship—whatever that work is, whether you're the CEO, or anything else. By way of example, in my book *God is My CEO,* I gave a story of ServiceMaster. Bill Pollard is CEO of a big cleaning service. He tells the story of Shirley, who has the unenviable job of cleaning toilets and post-surgical operating rooms. She could look at the job as a mere paycheck with no God involved. But the leaders helped her understand that work was to the glory of God and without her, the place wouldn't function. She knew that her cleaning enabled doctors to save people. So now, she's cleaning to honor God and what on the surface seems drudgery takes on great significance. We all have to do a lot mundane things, but God honors this and therein it has meaning."

Your Natural Strengths and Skills serve as your MAP

When I asked Julian to elaborate on the MAP concept, he said, "MAP stands for Motivated Abilities Pattern. This MAP helps you see the big picture of things that you do well in every aspect of life. In other words, God designed you with a unique set of abilities; you play it out all the time unconsciously. So, the MAP brings them to light. There are five pieces that help you see the big picture:

The **First is abilities,** your natural strengths, competencies, what you love to do.

The **Second is subject matter,** meaning what are the things you love to work with.

The **Third is circumstances**—what is the ideal setting that stimulates you to achieve? Some people do their best work alone; others love to work in groups or as part of a team.

The **Fourth is operating relationships,** i.e., in what ways do you interact with others in order to accomplish that meaningful result? So understand the nature of your relationships and what it is that you bring to the table.

The **Fifth** is that we all work for a pay-off, so what's the goal, what is the outcome that results from doing what you do?

Transform Pressure into Power

There's always a lot of advice around about changing stress into positive energy. But how, I asked Julian, can we do this? "This is important because we all face pressure and while no one wants to live under stress, it can also be a positive force. Negative stress derails us from our potential but positive stress stimulates our giftedness and lets us rise to the occasion. So transform this pressure into power. The first step is Awareness, your ability to see your world from God's perspective, which is important because a lot of times, we look only through our own eyes and it's easy to react negatively. Then stress gets the best of us. But when you see it from God's perspective you're seeing it from the possibility that maybe God is using this situation as part of His plan for you. And if you just trust in the Lord, He'll lead you to where you're supposed to be. The second thing is alignment. Transform your negative tendencies into a creative tension. Typically, when we're under stress, we worry and project. Alignment turns it into a creative tension, where you ask yourself, where are the opportunities for change? Live with the question rather than with the worry. This leads to the concept of adaptability, to resilience in uncertainty. So this is a big paradigm shift for many people and many leaders. We need to gain God's wisdom in the midst of crazy circumstances. Once we gain that insight, then we need to take action. So it's a two-step process."

Examine Your Definition of Success

I wanted to know Julian's definition of success. "It's all about relationships. The currency is relationships and not money." Not money! I was shocked. He went on, "What I mean by that is the value of who we are and who God has called us to be. One concept of prosperity is currency and material things, but the other is the concept of flourishing and abundance, or overflowing. From that standpoint it has a different meaning. For example, regarding *God is My CEO*, the world is going to define the success of that book as number of books sold. Great! From a financial standpoint the book has been successful. But ultimately what's best about the book is that it's still in print eleven years later and it has nothing to do with me anymore. It serves a purpose that's beyond me whether I'm around to enjoy it or not. One percent of the population has taken that book, been inspired by it and it perpetuates. And this is all about relationships. So the big questions are how are you impacting others, how are you adding to someone's life? It's good in business and it's good in life."

Chapter 14

The Future of Purpose-Inspired Marketing

The future is not some place we are going to, but one we are creating.
—Deborah James

The Law of Purpose

MY SECOND LEADERSHIP-DEFINING MOMENT happened during a conversation with Russell Simmons. He informed me that he wanted the RUSH employees to read *The Seven Spiritual Laws of Success: A Practical Guide to the Fulfillment of Your Dreams* by Deepak Chopra (New World Library, 1994). Not only that, but he wanted the employees to write a report regarding how they would use these universal principals in their personal and professional lives. To ensure this was woven through the fabric of the company, he also wanted the report to examine how the teachings would be manifest in our business environment and results. Spiritual reading requirement in business? It may seem odd at first, but looking back, I realize this was Simmons' way of getting his company connected to a higher, servant-style purpose.

Fast forward a number of years, and writing this chapter was a full circle moment. The memory of the assignment leapt top of mind as I was honored to connect with Mr. Deepak Chopra to discuss his view of applying the Law of Purpose in marketing and examine what's next for purpose-inspired marketers. I realized anew the importance of your view of the future in a way that matters to you. Only then will you behave differently in the present moment. The future, after all, creates the present.

I asked another great mind, Deepak Chopra, how he would encourage marketers to integrate the law of purpose in their day-to-day personal and professional lives. He replied that he does a special class with his Columbia MBA students on the premise that a brand must be a story, one with great spiritual and emotional appeal. "That story is about how can I serve, what is unique about us as a brand and what is the higher calling? People will buy a product or service because they find the story resonates with their spirit and their emotions. This is a phenomenon that cultural anthropologists call ritual action, which is the story they are buying. In the past, they would buy products with a story that was somehow breaking cultural norms: Volkswagen was the story of hippies, Harley-Davidson was the story of outlaw bikers, the Marlboro man was the story of the Lone Ranger. There was an emotional appeal to each of these stories because they appealed to something outside the cultural norm.

"But nowadays, rather than something outside the cultural norm, people are looking for how does that story impact the quality of life in society? At business school, one of the first things they teach you is that the purpose of brand or business is to improve shareholder value. I think that has to be redefined. The purpose of business is to serve society and improve the quality of life of the whole ecosystem, which of course includes people and the environment. You must look at your brand and ask what is unique about us, how can we serve, what are our special talents, our higher calling, and what is the story that will *resonate* with people. Once you have a resonating story, you have a very successful brand. If I am in a store and I am looking at two products of about the same price, the one that has the more appealing story is the one I'm going to buy." Does it get much clearer than that?

"In the future, connect your personal life story to be an agent of change to create the world you want to live in. Become, in Gandhi's words, the change that you want to see in the world. Ask, how is my personal story connected to my professional story? My students at Columbia are doing an incredible job at this. If you are going with purpose," Chopra told me in a soft but firm voice, "you will make a profit and the impact will be long lasting. But if you're going for profit only, you may succeed in the short run but in the long run you'll fizzle out and lose energy. The trend is so much more for purpose-inspired marketing that without it; you won't be part of the mainstream anymore."

The Future of Purpose-Inspired Marketing

Then, I wanted to know if he could provide any insight around what he feels the future trends for business that are up to the challenge of becoming purpose inspired from the inside out.

He encourages business leaders to take a macro look at the world's *wellbeing*. He says, what's happening in the world, or in society, is a reflection of the wellbeing in the following areas: career, financial, social, physical, emotional, and spiritual. If you are to monitor anything in society, your best indicator—you guessed it—is to monitor wellbeing. As Chopra says, "It correlates with hospital admissions, with crime, with violence, with quality of leadership, with success of business and financial markets."

He challenges his Columbia MBA students, to see purpose-driven marketing as posing the questions, "Which sector of the world or community or population's wellbeing will be enhanced by your business? Will it improve people's careers? Will it create better communities? Will it engage people socially in helping to create a peaceful, just, sustainable and healthy environment? If it does, then your business is going to be successful."

Yes, these questions have infiltrated the hallowed halls of major business schools, as yet another factor that will profoundly affect the future of purpose-driven marketing. Communicating your ideals to engage not just customers, but employees, too, is the surefire way to go. And, remember, shared fundamental values engender one element above all: trust.

As famed global marketing officer Jim Stengel says in his bestselling book *Grow*: "Trust, honesty, respect, caring, warmth and humor aren't the criteria most companies use to develop and measure their communications. But they are the criteria most successful businesses use." These are *visionary* concepts that will change your company at every level.

Take Close Note, Deepak Chopra predicts . . .

"In years to come, you'll just plain be out of date if you're not contributing in some way to the wellbeing of society."

I'm a firm believer, as said, that the future is created in the present. And I think Chopra was very intentional about tomorrow's possibilities he was creating with this challenge: "In the future, the marketing person who's creating a global campaign for all multinational companies to donate one percent of all profits to a particular cause, will be key. Should that become a trend, you can be sure that if every Fortune 500 company contributed one percent of its profits to a particular cause, you could eliminate world hunger, you could provide jobs, you would decrease addictions and addictive behaviors, and *that* is purpose-inspired marketing. The vision is more than sufficient to inspire the imagination."

Serve the world through your brand purpose

That's what Deepak Chopra is teaching his business students at Columbia—that when you create a business you have to consider (that word again) the *wellbeing* of all these different constituencies: your employees, your customers, and everyone else who is affected by your business. There is, he insists, a correlation between the wellbeing of the people in the business, and not just the profit of the business, but also how it is impacting sustainability, impacting violence in the community, and in the ecosystem. How is it impacting nurturing of relationships and how is it enhancing the quality of life in general? To illustrate this, he says,

"We also bring in entrepreneurs who are good examples, such as rapper 50 Cent and his energy drink Street King. For every bottle that's sold, a child is fed in Africa. This is how he's actually marketing his energy drink, which is an indicator of urban consumers' receptivity to taking greater responsibility. In addition," Chopra goes on to say, "I had a woman in my course who does lingerie shows with supermodels. The lingerie is auctioned at the site, the Seven Bar Foundation (sevenbarfoundation. org), with the proceeds going to microfinance poor women."

Another example of a purpose–inspired initiative that Chopra encouraged us to keep a close eye on is AHAlife.com where they have the Karma Club. All the products that are sold enhance the lives of people who are connected to the product. Curious to learn more, I went to the AHAlife.com website where I learned that the purpose of the site is to help people find unique gifts and that each product sold on the site benefits a particular cause.

Employee engagement is critical link

Another key nugget of wisdom Chopra shared is to keep employee engagement at the forefront of the purpose equation. For one thing, employee involvement in causes has grown tremendously by the availability of information on the internet. As employees expect choice and access in their giving and volunteering, management has come to realize that not only individual employees but regional and retail teams, indeed entire divisions, are getting more input into company-endorsed social action, and have begun to share on social media. The result is significantly increased rates of charitable donations, volunteering, meeting attendance, events, and the undertaking of leadership roles. Engage them and have them take ownership in your brand's greater purpose; give them the tools to co-create with you to activate their social networks. The strongest advocate, influencer, word-of-mouth driver for you is a fulfilled employee who has a shared vision with your company's greater purpose.

How engaged are your employees? As Deepak Chopra told me, "The

Leadership should place their employees' wellbeing first. If employees are disengaged, the difference between disengagement and active disengagement means just punching the clock for the former and for the latter, the actively disengaged has people making others unhappy. If 25 to 45 percent of the workforce is actively disengaged, that costs the U.S. economy $280 billion a year. This is because they are not being nurtured in terms of using their strengths or in terms of social interactions."

Great leaders have mastered the combination to unlock the potential of all their employees. Chopra, a man who has been a seeker all his life, is inspired to write what he does. Ever the seeker, his path has led him to become an inspired teacher, not always noncontroversial. But, as Albert Einstein said, "Great spirits have always encountered violent opposition from mediocre minds." Chopra has inspired positive, real changes in many people's lives.

Key Trends

The future of purpose-driven marketing, in a world where purpose and profit are no longer mutually exclusive, will be defined by many different elements, but these over-arching trends especially stand out:

Engage employees and consumers

The first, engaging employees and consumers, has everything to do with narrative, as we've seen throughout this book. But it's also important to remember, especially in today's recovering economy, the concept of *re-engaging* those same two entities.

Engaging employees is about much more than passive company logo mouse pads, coffee mugs, and tee shirts. Internal branding has to take the form of a dynamic method of aligning your employees to your company's mission, to its purpose, and to its vision. Think of everything as communicating—your stories, your expression, even your office layout and dress code. Nothing is trivial. All employees within the company need constant reinforcement regarding implicit messages as to what your brand stands for and further, how that translates into daily transactions.

Consistent internal brand building is creative. After all, employees wear two hats: they are consumers, too. Their brand expectations are also high and influenced by their experiences with other brands. The marketing department can divide your staff and create targeted communication plans for each segment. Also, key success metrics play a role by showing whether or not you're headed in the right direction.

As Deepak Chopra, among others, believes, emotional as well as rational understanding must be successfully targeted. When both aspects are included, only then can campaigns change behavior. And while it may seem obvious, too many companies frequently overlook an important fact. Unless employees talk and act consistently with your brand's message, all your external branding activity may well come to naught.

No one argues with the importance of strong training. However, while traditional employee engagement emphasizes communication and intrinsic motivation via rewards and recognition, the focus now needs to be on understanding that people are more committed to ideas that they helped to develop. So what exactly is the goal? Developing a workforce that is motivated to deliver remarkable consumer experiences.

Corporate Social Responsibility as core ethos

Corporate Social Responsibility, commonly known as CSR, is a phrase you've heard a lot, but what exactly does it mean? The best, and simplest, definition is that CSR is about how corporations manage their business procedures to produce an overall positive impact on society.

From Hennessy to Wells Fargo to Bounty and more, we've seen ample illustrations of what this means. Companies need to respond to two sides of their operations, both the quality of their management (people and processes, the *inner circle*) and the quantity of their impact on society in diverse areas. Today, outside stakeholders are showing increased interest in a company's activity. Most view the *outer*

The Business in Society

circle—what the company has actually done in terms of products and services. Along with past financial performance, financial analysts are keenly interested in management quality as a bellwether for future performance.

Ethical behavior and contributions to economic development, and improvement of the workforce's quality of life figure prominently in the definition of CSR, along with positive impact on the local community and society at large. Think in terms of capacity building for sustainable livelihoods, something Deepak Chopra has emphasized. When cultural differences are appreciated and respected, business opportunities emerge, especially in building employee skills, and the community as a whole.

Many people think of CSR as a philanthropic model. Companies make profits, pay taxes, then give a share of those profits to support charitable causes. It is negative to the company's image to be seen as gaining any benefit from their charitable giving. But another model is far more concerned with operating the core business in a socially responsible fashion—balanced by investment based on solid business reasons. CSR thus becomes a key part of the wealth creation process. If properly managed, the competitiveness of the business is boosted, and the inherent value of wealth creation to society is significantly enlarged. Business for Social Responsibility (BSR), a global partner for responsible business leaders, defines Corporate Social Responsibility as "Operating a business in a manner that meets or exceeds the ethical, legal, commercial and public expectations that society has of business." Amen.

Purpose as articulation of brand's reason for being

What does branding actually do? It saves us from living in a world of generic products traded solely on price, according to the laws of supply and demand. What a bland world that would be. Branding enables companies to provide something we can aspire to, something to help in cultivating our own identities in the process. And don't brands enrich our lives? Think about it. With basic needs met, brands add color and personality, fun and inspiration, to the necessary act of making purchasing decisions.

Consider some of the world's great brands, such as Apple, IBM, Coca-Cola, American Express, and Sony. They not only garner respect from consumers worldwide, but, as author Paul Stobart puts it, "strong relevant identities for specific branded offerings enhance a firms' profitability and influence in terms of competition in its industry. Brands also greatly facilitate the introduction of additional products by companies in possession of popular brands."[1]

If I were to point to one single example of a sublimely articulated purpose for a brand's reason for being, I'd turn to page 106 of a book already cited in these pages: Tom Asacker's *Opportunity Screams* (Paramount Market Publishing, Inc., 2011). Asacker writes:

The marketplace is an ever-shifting, always evolving social organization.

Any idea can be turned into a protagonist for societal change and create feelings of shared passion. But to do so, you have to elevate your idea to something meaningful, something with soul. And then you have to energize it and bring it to life in a way that *stimulates* interaction and sharing, and which enhances the link between people's lives and your idea.

Unilever *elevated* Dove from a cleansing and moisturizing idea to a statement about beauty in an age of Photoshop and cosmetic surgery. Its *Campaign for Real Beauty* is about celebrating the natural beauty of all women and inspiring them to feel good about themselves. The company then *stimulated* conversations and fed people's social hungers with an incredibly powerful video called Dove Evolution and with follow-on social catalysts in the form of online films, print advertisements, billboards, workshops, sleepover events, and even a book and a play.

So there's soap. Google did it with 1s and 0s. Red Bull did it with a foul-tasting beverage. Apple did it with an MP3 player. Nike did it with a sneaker.

This is brand purpose articulation taken to its highest degree and what you have to aim for in your own endeavors. And never forget: to serve is your highest purpose. In order to get, you have to serve others.

People must remain as the center of purpose

But what about engaging consumers in this process? Well, MSL has developed an exciting new initiative called PURPLE, an acronym for PURPOSE + PEOPLE. Purpose is now about creating shared value above all.

How Can Companies Become Purpose Led?

Purpose is about Opportunity and Potential. People Make it Real with their Insights.

The specific steps for companies to take in order to become purpose led are and always will be:

1. Create collaborative social innovation

2. Initiate grassroots change movements

3. Create a shared purpose to inspire people

4. Create platforms to organize people

5. Create programs to energize people

6. Tell stories to spark participation and action

Engaging consumers in a purpose is essential because the ship won't sail without your customers on board. People, I repeat, must remain as the center of purpose. It's been a pleasure for me to share with you key learnings I've obtained over the past 10 years. I'm grateful for all of the amazing experts that shared their wisdom and insight for the creation of this book. I hope the trends and key learning prove valuable to you. As I wind down, I'm excited about the potential for you and for what's next in your personal and professional life. The world is filled with opportunities and the world is hungry for your "personal"/"professional" brand purpose to shine.

This is a great time to be alive—whether you are a purpose-inspired college student, employee, business leader, marketer, or CEO. The job title doesn't matter. There exists an opportunity for your brand purpose to come to life. Remember: every day you have the power to align your purpose to serve others. As you do that, get ready for a life filled with meaning and a company built on a strong sense of the same. Look at what happened when Walt Disney got in tune with his purpose, when Steve Jobs got in tune, when Oprah got in tune. So get ready and don't forget to enjoy the journey, to have fun as you bring forth your unique creative gifts. May you feel your purpose come to life one idea, one product, one service, or one campaign at time.

Until the next time . . .
Live on Purpose,
Teneshia

Acknowledgments

THIS JOURNEY has been filled with supportive team members, with family and friends along the way—to all of them I express my sincere gratitude.

First, to my higher power and source, my Lord God—I thank you for guiding me through this 10-year dream path. I'm eternally grateful to serve as your vessel and co-create with you in this journey called life. May you remain my source, my anchor and my inner purpose compass.

To my husband, Michael Charles Warner, who from our first date reflected nothing back to me but possibility, with whom I have felt safe to share every dream. You are my best friend and my beloved.

To the entire Egami team past, present and future: Adrienne Alexander, Allison Rhone, Shantelle Guyton, Adair Curtis, Ashley Brabham, Sheryl Wesley, Tuwisha Rogers, Janice Torres, Jessyka Castillo, Dupe Ajene, Jason Draper, Tasha Stoute, Claudine Moore, Khelli Dowdell, Kapri Jackson, LL Business Management and more. Thank you for your hard work, dedication and your "purpose inspired" ideas. May we continue to serve the world one campaign at a time.

To the MSL family: Tony Cofone, Renee Wilson, Joel Curran, Scott Beaudin, Caryn Carmer, Daphne Hoytt, Brian Williams, LeAnne Attelony, Patricia Hallock, Michael Echter, Ofer Erenfeld, Erin Ortiz, Carmen Jurden and the entire gang. I'm extremely grateful to all of you for our five-years-and-growing partnership.

To my fabulous interviewees: Russell Simmons, Deepak Chopra,

Belinda Wilson, Beverly Bond, Bevy Smith, Fernando Molinar, Jenay Alejandro, Lisa Stone, Monica McCluney, Martin Ankamah, Phillip Bloch, Troy Brown, my cousin Kennedy and Verna Coleman-Hagler. My special thanks to all of you for your vision and perspective. Special shout out to Scott Beaudoin, MSL NY consumer practice director—thanks for being an inspiration. This book would not have been possible without your valuable insight and guidance. I look forward to delivering purpose-inspired campaigns with you and the MSL Purpose team for many years to come.

To my literary team: Paramount Market Publishing, Inc., thanks for believing. To Doris Walsh and Jim Madden, thank you for your patience and for your willingness to take a chance on me. To my agent, Regina Brooks, you have been a friend, a coach and counselor throughout this process. To my editor, Phoebe Collins, you are my angel; thanks for partnering with me on this journey and serving as an instrument for my voice.

To our clients: Russell Simmons' RUSH Communication, Jostens, P&G, Bounty, My Black is Beautiful, Verizon Wireless, KFC, Heineken, Hennessy, and the list goes on. Thank you for the chance to partner with you on purpose-inspired marketing initiatives.

To my mother, Carolyn Hearns: Thank you, Mom, for your friendship and encouragement. I could not have designed a better mother. To my grandparents, Coley and Northa Hearns, I love you and treasure your ongoing source of wisdom. To my dad, Robert Earl Jackson: Thanks for giving me your drive and hustle. To my niece, Alexusia Hearns: You are my inspiration. To the Warners, Bria and Amber: Thank you for being an amazing support system. To Joseph Almond: Thanks for inspiring me to DREAM. And special thanks to the Jackson and Jones-Lewis families.

To the Johnsons, Chelle, Celeste, and Chester: We are the Fabulous Five and God gave us a special blessing when he gave us family. You all will forever be my unconditional rock.

To my college family: Chelonnda, Courtney, Monica, Kim Carr, Kelli and Karen: thanks for the blessings of sisterhood and friendship. To LoveWorks: Monica and Vince, may your purpose blossom. To the

One Arm Up Crew: Tiffany, Jamese, Kronsky, Meredith and Jennifer, to Angianein Felder, Toby Robbins, Sharrie Warner, and Lisa Gilbertson. We have gone from club partying, to corporate offices, to marriage and for some of you to motherhood. God truly gave us a gift in when he created friendship.

To my New York friends, especially My RUSH family: Allison Rhone, Freny Baloyo, Tina Lee, Daphne Hoytt, Phillip Sontag, Laura Hall, Tai Beauchamp, Valiesha Butterfield, Jo Jo Brimm, so blessed to have all of you in my life. To Sylvia High—you are my muse.

To the Pine Mountain's Mountain Top Inn cabin staff: Thanks for providing me a peaceful place to write and give birth to this idea. Look out for the DreamMaker Cabin @ Mountain Inn, brought to you by Egami. To all my organizations that hold me down: To Momentum Education, Ad Color Awards, Harlem Fashion Row, Black Girls Rock!, WEEN, and Delta Sigma Theta and more. May your missions continue to serve the world.

To my Glam Squad Marcus Ivory (stylist), Jennifer Cooper (photographer) and makeup artist (Joanna Smikin): thank you for an amazing cover shoot. Designers who worked on the cover: Kwaku at One Design and Carmen Jurden.

To my Angels: Thank you, Aunt Margaret, you are eternally a source of inspiration for me. Uncle Rochestor, thank you for the belief. To Jerold Hearns: Remember there is no me without you, so you live on. To Yoshi Warner (my doggie): Thanks for an amazing seven years.

To all others that I may have missed, you are in my heart and I express to you gratitude for your friendship, support and belief.

UNTIL THE NEXT TIME,
TENESHIA JACKSON WARNER
NEW YORK CITY, 2012

Other books we admire on the subject of purpose & multicultural marketing

It's Not What You Sell, It's What You Stand For: Why Every Extraordinary Business Is Driven by Purpose, Roy Spence

Good to Great: Why Some Companies Make the Leap . . . and Other's Don't, Jim Collins

GROW: How Ideals Power Growth and Profit at the World's Greatest Companies, Jim Stengal

Opportunity Screams: Unlocking Hearts and Minds in Today's Idea Economy, Tom Asacker

Black Still Matters in Marketing: Why Increasing Your Cultural IQ about Black America is Critical to Your Business and Your Brand, Pepper Miller

The Tanning of America: How Hip-Hop Created a Culture That Rewrote the Rules of the New Economy, Steve Stoute

Under the Influence: Tracing the Hip-Hop Generation's Impact on Brands, Sports, & Pop Culture, Eric O. Patton

Hispanic Customers for Life, M. Isabel Valdés

The Seven Spiritual Laws of Success: A Practical Guide to the Fulfillment of Your Dreams, Deepak Chopra

The Alchemist, Paulo Coelho and Alan R. Clarke

The Dream Giver, Bruce Wilkinson, David Kopp and Heather Kopp

Super Rich: A Guide to Having It All, Russell Simmons

The Purpose Driven Life: What on Earth am I Here For? Rick Warren

Index

About Teneshia Jackson Warner and Egami Consulting Group

TENESHIA JACKSON WARNER is an award-winning multicultural marketing expert. She began her career as a mentee of the globally successful innovator, entrepreneur and hip-hop mogul, Russell Simmons where she was the General Manager of Rush Communications. Encouraged by Russell, Teneshia embarked upon her own entrepreneurial path, and founded Egami Consulting Group (Egami) in 2003.

Egami is now an award-winning multicultural marketing firm and under her leadership, Egami formed a strategic partnership with the world's third largest communications firm MSLGroup, a Publicis Groupe global engagement firm, and acts as their exclusive diversity marketing partner working to deliver multicultural marketing solutions to their client network. Together they have delivered award-winning client work for leading brands such as P&G's Bounty and My Black is Beautiful, Verizon Wireless, Hennessy, Heineken, Dasani, General Motors, Western Union and KFC.

Teneshia has won several business awards including the coveted Black Enterprise "Rising Star 40 and Under" in 2012 and in 2010, she was also recognized by The Network Journal "Forty Under 40 Award" for U.S. African-American achievers. She was born in Marianna, Florida, and raised in Dothan, Alabama, and is a graduate of HBCU, Alabama A&M University, where she received a BS in Computer Science and minor in Communications. She is married to Mike Warner who, as her business partner, serves as Egami's Chief Operating Officer.

Egami Consulting Group is an award-winning, WBENC and NMSDC, certified woman-owned minority marketing firm specializing in linking brands to urban and multicultural consumers via inspirational platforms. Founded in 2003 by award-winning marketing expert Teneshia Jackson Warner, Egami provides brands ways to Inspire, Connect, and Activate consumers through innovative marketing campaigns, strategic partnerships, custom community programs, and/or new products. The firm leverages insights and it's authentic connection to urban culture and multicultural audiences to create unique marketing strategies that Activate consumers. Egami has worked with many leading brands including Fortune 100 companies. Among past and present clients include Proctor & Gamble, Verizon Wireless, Bounty, YUM! Brands/ Kentucky Fried Chicken, Jostens, Hennessy, Heineken, Eli Lilly and more.

For those interested in EGAMI/MSLGROUP Purpose offering, please contact us at:

Teneshia Jackson Warner
> CEO & Founder, EGAMI Consulting Group
> info@egamiconsulting.com
>
> www.egamiconsulting.com.

Scott Beaudoin
> SVP, NYC Consumer Marketing Practice Director; Global Director, PurPle (Purpose + People) MSL New York
> scott.beaudoin@mslgroup.com